BEGINNER'S GUIDE TO

Attracting Birds

to your backyard

Contributing Writer
Mary Heimerdinger Clench, Ph.D.

Consultant
Sally Hoyt Spofford, Ph.D.

PUBLICATIONS INTERNATIONAL, LTD.

Mary Heimerdinger Clench is the former director of the National Audubon Society; editor of *The Living Bird,* Cornell University; associate curator of birds, Carnegie Museum of Natural History; and president of the Wilson Ornithological Society. She holds a Ph.D. in biology from Yale University.

Sally Hoyt Spofford is a retired ornithologist whose articles have appeared in a variety of ornithological journals. She has been a guest on 200 radio programs, a bird-bander for 40 years, and was assistant to the director of Cornell Laboratory of Ornithology for 10 years.

TABLE OF CONTENTS

Introduction

Attracting wild birds to your backyard can greatly increase your enjoyment of the natural world. You will find the birds that live in or visit your yard to be colorful, interesting guests. By providing food, water, and nesting places, you can ensure many hours of enjoyment for yourself and your family, and you'll also have the satisfaction of knowing you are helping the native wildlife.

If not many birds seem to be in your area, try a simple experiment: scatter some mixed seed (available from any grocery store) and bits of white bread on the ground. You almost surely will soon see birds you never suspected were in the neighborhood, as more and more, in a variety of species, come to enjoy your generosity. Your efforts will be especially successful if you start feeding in the fall because that is usually when birds are moving about, looking for an area with a good supply of food, water, and shelter to settle for the winter. The birds may be both young ones that were hatched locally and newly arrived species that have migrated from their more northern breeding grounds. Unless you offer them some simple hospitality, though, you probably won't have the chance to enjoy the company of many of these winged creatures.

A robin clings to the rim of a birdbath.

A Mountain Chickadee takes refuge in a dense evergreen.

In time you'll notice that different species have different habits and food preferences. Some birds will feed only on the ground, but others prefer a hanging feeder. Some eat only small seeds, while others pick out the sunflower seeds from a mixture. A few species may be too shy to come close to the house, but some will crowd around a feeder on the windowsill. It is best for the birds and for you to have several feeders stocked with different foods to cater to the widest possible variety of your wild "clientele."

If you live in an arid climate, or one that is dry during certain seasons of the year, many kinds of birds — including those that are not interested in your feeders — will come to your yard for water. A brimming birdbath, especially if it has water moving or dripping in it, is a major attraction for *every* bird in the area.

More birds will stay in your yard for the winter if you can offer shelter such as evergreens or brush piles for roosting away from the wind and cold. In the spring and summer, you can get birds to set up house in your yard if you provide nesting places like shrubbery and nest boxes.

As the birds arrive in greater and greater number, you may find yourself wanting to know more about them. The last part of this book contains pictures and information on birds that often take advantage of human hospitality. Eventually, you may want to get a field guide to the birds of your region of the country so that you can identify everything you see. Start a list of the birds you attract to the feeders and water; it's surprising how impressively long such a list can grow. Many people keep detailed journals of the birdlife in their yards, making notes on feeding habits, courtship rituals, nesting activity, and other fascinating behaviors. And if photography is your hobby, what better opportunity to capture birds and other backyard wildlife on film than by attracting them close to your window?

Creating a successful habitat for birds is a hobby that almost everyone has the time, money, and resources to pursue. Millions of Americans have already learned how much pleasure they get from their backyard birds. We hope you will, too.

Above, left: *A robin tends to its young in a backyard tree.* Left: *The cardinal is just one of the dozens of bird species you can attract to your yard.*

CHAPTER 1

Food in Winter

There is no wrong time to set up a feeding station for birds. They can be found in virtually every part of the country at any time of year, and they will always be willing to take advantage of a steady food source. Perhaps the best time to begin, though, is in early fall, when bird populations and activity are both at a peak. You'll have greater numbers of birds in your general vicinity, and they'll all be looking for food. Some will simply be stocking up before the next leg of their migration; they may use your feeders only once and then move on. But others, the ones that winter in your area, will be carefully searching out the feeding grounds that will sustain them in the coming months.

Once birds have found food, water, and appropriate shelter for the winter, they usually will settle down in the vicinity. They may move from feeder to feeder throughout a neighborhood, and they will likely seek variety in nearby fields and woods with natural foods not covered by ice and snow, but they will always come back to the feeders that first attracted them. So along with your enjoyment comes a responsibility. In feeding and watering birds in winter, there is one cardinal rule (pun intended): Once you begin, *continue feeding until spring,* when natural foods and water again become abundant. If you take a vacation or are away from home for several days after you have begun to feed the birds in winter, ask a neighbor to keep your feeders and birdbaths well supplied in your absence. If you don't, the birds may not starve, but they will suffer. They'll have to look for a more reliable source, and their diet will be limited in the meantime. The birds are also unlikely to return to your feeders after you get back home because they will have resettled at someone else's.

Birds relish many kinds of food in winter. The following discussion of feed includes types that are commonly available, well liked, and very nutritious. It also cautions you on what to avoid.

SEEDS AND GRAINS
Mixed wild bird seed is widely available and eaten by most winter birds. Good commercial mixtures provide a balanced diet with sufficient portions of fats, proteins, and carbohydrates. The best mixtures contain seeds with high fat content, which birds particularly like and which are especially important in cold weather.

Sunflower seed is easily the most popular form of feed. Black-oil sunflower seed, also called perodovic sunflower or oilseed, and striped sunflower seed are both eagerly eaten by most of the larger birds that visit feeders. White millet or white proso millet is the best all-around seed for small birds, and safflower seed is especially liked by cardinals, but not by sparrows, blackbirds, or squirrels.

Sunflower seed is far and away the most universally liked food you can offer to your birds, and it's also highly nutritious. It will always draw a variety of larger species for you to enjoy.

Top: *This feeder contains mixed seed. Mixes can be economical and well liked by many birds, but you have to know how to shop for them; check the contents to be sure that your visitors will eat the fillers.* Above: *A Carolina Chickadee retreats to the solitude of a snow-dusted evergreen where it will enjoy the prize held in its beak.*

Mixtures also almost invariably include cheaper seeds that are less desirable for most birds, although some of these fillers may be liked by certain individual species. Cheap (and sometimes not-so-cheap) mixes may have a lot of things such as leftover garden seed that none of your birds will eat. You don't want to keep buying a mixture that mostly remains on the ground uneaten. Acceptable fillers include cracked corn, hulled or whole wheat, oats, and rice.

Try to avoid mixes containing large amounts of rape seed, which canaries like but wild birds usually don't. Flax, buckwheat, and millet other than the white proso millet are inexpensive fillers, but they are not very appealing to the birds.

Also avoid seed mixtures that contain grit unless your region is entirely snow-covered all winter. Birds have no teeth, so they need the grit to help grind up the food in their gizzards. If they can find it naturally from bare ground, though, it is nonsense to pay seed prices for sand and gravel. Crushed eggshells are another alternative. They offer a good source of calcium and are eagerly eaten as grit.

Thistle or niger is an excellent specialty seed that seems to make goldfinches, siskins, and redpolls appear out of thin air to line up at the feeder. Thistle is best dispensed from its own type of feeder with tiny slit holes that allow small birds with pointed bills to extract the small and very expensive seed with a minimum of waste. Another effective feeder for this seed is a thistle stocking, which is made of fine nylon netting.

A mesh bag makes the perfect dispenser for fat-based mixtures; it's functional, inexpensive, and disposable.

A Red-bellied Woodpecker clings to this homemade basket feeder and feasts diligently at the suet it contains.

Peanut kernels are another excellent food if you are sure they are not rancid, as they may be in old mixtures. Peanut *bits,* however, are a magnet for starlings, and many people try to avoid these greedy and quarrelsome birds. Starlings are relatively large, with comparably large appetites. What's worse is that they're also quite aggressive, and they will not hesitate to drive away the smaller, often more attractive species from your yard. Peanuts in the shell can be strung on a string and hung up for titmice and chickadees. These small birds make a delightful sight as they cling to the shell and pound their way into the nut. Most other kinds of nuts are also good, but more expensive — local prices may make the decision for you.

A sensible approach to feeding seed is to begin with a mixture, but watch to see which birds eat what and how much is wasted. If you find that an effective mix is not available, you may then decide it is more economical to buy only the most readily eaten seeds, usually at a feed store or by specialty mail order. If a good mixture is available locally from a nature or garden center or from a grocery or hardware store, filling one large hopper feeder with the mix, another perhaps smaller feeder with sunflower seed, and a third special tube feeder with thistle should keep most birds content at minimum cost. With a good mixture, the less desirable seeds that are flicked out of the hopper feeder will usually be cleaned up by the birds that feed on the ground, and they count, too.

FAT
Many bird species depend on high-energy fats as a major part of their diet in winter. Beef suet is well liked and inexpensive. Butchers always have it and supermarkets commonly sell packages of it in their meat cases, or you can trim thick fat from uncooked beef cuts and store it in the freezer. Offer the suet to birds in several ways. Woodpeckers, chickadees, and other good clingers will enjoy raw chunks hung up in a mesh bag. Ground suet put out on a shelf feeder will draw a wider variety of species, including juncos and many sparrows or even wintering warblers. Beef suet may also be melted and added to other foods (see "Bird Puddings" on following page).

Most birds dislike lamb fat, even in trace amounts. Very salty fats (especially bacon) may be liked, but they should be blended in small amounts with other foods. Peanut butter is greatly favored, but many experts say it *must* be mixed with something like cornmeal to eliminate its stickiness in the belief that peanut butter can kill if it lodges in a bird's throat.

These foods can be laid out for your birds in a variety of ways. Hang suet or fat mixtures in mesh bags (such as onion bags from the grocery) or in wire baskets. Fat or fatty mixtures can also be smeared in pine cones or on rough tree trunks, put in coconut shell halves, or in holes drilled in small logs. The idea is to keep squirrels, starlings, or other "food hogs" from carrying off the whole lot at once.

FRUITS

Raisins (chopped up for the small birds) will attract fruit-eaters such as area mockingbirds, robins, and other thrushes to your yard. Orioles and some others also relish oranges, grapes, cherries, apples, ripe bananas, or almost any sweet fruit — fresh or frozen — cut in small pieces and put out on a flat tray feeder. A natural raw coconut, split open and hung up in its shell, will be enjoyed by many birds. Do not feed dry or shredded "fresh" coconut by itself because it will swell in a bird's stomach; it can be mixed into other foods.

BIRD PUDDINGS

For those of you who might like to cook for your birds, homemade mixtures can be easy, fun, and very effective in attracting birds that like suet to your yard. The basic recipe consists of cooked cereal with melted fat and enough dry material added to form a solid mass, but the possible variations are limited only by your imagination. Here's a simple one: Cook 2 cups of oatmeal. While it is still hot, stir in and melt 1 pound of lard or suet and 1 cup of peanut butter; you may also add leftover drippings from meat you have cooked. Add any combination of cornmeal, bread crumbs, chopped unsalted nuts, uncooked oatmeal, raisins or currants, and crushed dog biscuits. Stir until stiff. Form into large balls or pour into foil cupcake pans. Keep refrigerated or frozen until you're ready to put it out.

Remember that these treats are as desirable to squirrels, raccoons, and other large pests as they are to the birds. If you're going to put puddings out, be sure that you make them inaccessible to the other creatures or your birds will never get to taste your efforts. Chapter 6, Common Problems and What to Do about Them, provides guidelines on how to pest-proof your feeders.

WHITE BREAD

White bread is attractive to almost all species, and it helps draw birds to a new feeding area. Stale cake, cookies, doughnuts, and other breadstuffs are all liked, but oddly enough, dark breads are usually left untouched. White breads are not, however, a well-balanced diet and should not be the only food offered. They are relished by nuisance species, too, so be warned!

KITCHEN SCRAPS

Once birds are used to a feeder, they will eat a surprising variety of kitchen leftovers: cooked pasta or rice, apple peelings, cheese crumbs, melon and squash seeds (chopped open), stale cereals, and many other scraps. Experiment with small amounts and remove anything the birds don't eat quickly. Especially when on the ground, kitchen scraps spoil rapidly, and they can also attract rats or stray dogs. Do not put out anything very salty or highly seasoned.

Shelf feeders are varied in design and use: a flicker (top) enjoys suet laid out on a tree stump while a grosbeak (above) picks at seed.

FEEDERS

Feeders can be simple or fancy, homemade or store-bought. For your benefit, they should be easy to fill and clean. For the birds' benefit, they should keep food dry and protected from the weather; sodden food spoils and causes disease.

Shelf feeders or *bird tables* hold limited amounts of food and must be stocked daily. They are the most versatile feeders because they can hold almost any sort of food, but they require more attention because they must be filled often, preferably at the same time each day. It may be most convenient to have a shelf feeder on a windowsill, where it can be reached through a window. Windowsill feeders are best if they have clear plastic roofs, so feeding birds can be seen and enjoyed from behind the window curtain. Some birds, however, may be too timid to come close to a house, at least at first, but will readily use a tall shelf feeder at the back of the yard. Once the birds are used to this or any kind of feeder, it may gradually be moved closer for better viewing.

Hopper feeders can be used only for seed, but they are convenient because they hold several days' supply, dispensing seed only as it is eaten and protecting it from wind and water. Large hoppers are the most common type of feeder, usually used for seed mixtures. Smaller hoppers are often specialized, designed for agile clinging birds like titmice, chickadees, and nuthatches and stocked with these species' favorite seed.

Suet feeders are used for the high-fat soft foods relished by those species that feed on insects in the summer and non-seed foods in winter. The simplest suet feeder is a coarse-mesh plastic bag such as those in which citrus fruits or onions usually are sold. More durable suet holders may be made of wire mesh coated with plastic.

Ground feeding may be accomplished by putting a wide board or other easily cleaned surface on the ground, either in the open or sheltered under some sort of roof, and stocking it as you would a shelf feeder. Usually, though, enough food is naturally spilled by birds visiting shelf or hopper feeders to supply the ground-feeding species such as doves. The ground under such feeders needs regular cleaning to prevent disease organisms such as *Salmonella* and *Aspergillus* from growing on the accumulated seed hulls, wasted seed, and droppings.

Feeder locations should be chosen first for the *birds'* benefit and second for yours. Depending on the severity of your winters, sites should be sheltered, as in the lee of a house or near a dense group of evergreens. Feeders also should be positioned to provide safety from predators. Trees, shrubs, fences, or clotheslines, for example, should be a few feet away to be used as perches, with dense protective cover like a brush pile nearby. Hanging feeders are best suspended five to six feet off the ground to be out of reach from jumping cats and squirrels. Feeders on poles should be a similar height. Remember that a thick snow cover can quickly bring a feeder within reach of predators, so raise the feeder if conditions warrant. Also try not to crowd feeders into a small area; when they are well spaced, the more timid birds have a chance to feed undisturbed.

Top: *Birds that will feed on the ground will usually find all they can eat below a hanging feeder. Even with a light covering of snow, this junco has still turned up some seed.* Above: *A Rufous-sided Towhee cracks open a sunflower seed with its powerful beak.*

Food in Summer

Summer brings new species to your area.

Even in the summer when their preferred diet of insects is widely available, woodpeckers will still come to your feeders as long as you keep them stocked.

Birds need a plentiful food supply in winter more than at any other time. But when spring arrives, the situation changes. Insects, buds, early fruits, and seeds appear, and the birds you have been feeding all winter no longer need your efforts. Should you stop? Many people do, knowing that supplementary feeding is no longer necessary. Some even have the attitude that the winter freeloaders should now repay the debt by eating bugs. But if you want to continue enjoying as well as helping some of your backyard birds, it won't hurt to continue feeding them.

Most of the backyard residents will appreciate the variety that your handouts offer, and many of the birds can use the help in feeding their hungry young. For you, summer feeding also offers some opportunities not available during winter. One of the most delightful sights in the bird-watching world is a family of just-fledged nestlings being brought to your feeder by their parents. You may meet several new species that have returned to your area to breed after spending the winter farther south.

In general, you can continue the feeding already established during winter, but keep an eye out for any changes in what is and isn't eaten. Depending on how much of what is consumed, you can alter the feed you serve. When birds spread out to begin nesting, you won't have the hungry mobs you had all winter. You'll be able to cut back on the amounts of almost everything. Also, some species will have left for their more northern breeding grounds, so you can stop providing their special foods.

The single most important thing to remember when feeding birds in summer is that keeping the feeding area clean is absolutely *critical.* When temperatures are high, uneaten seed, discarded hulls and other scraps, and bird droppings are a breeding ground for disabling and deadly diseases. Extreme care must be used with high-fat foods. Perishables like suet and table scraps have to be watched carefully and removed *before* they spoil. Grind the suet into small bits and put out a small amount at a time, no more than will be eaten up in an hour or two. If this is done at the same time each day, you may be surprised at who learns to come down for the suet. Perhaps you'll see warblers, tanagers, and orioles that normally don't leave their treetops during summer.

NECTAR

One special feeding technique, useful in winter only to those who live in the southernmost states but available to everyone in summer, is how to attract hummingbirds. Planting your garden with flowers that offer a good supply of nectar is the best way, but offering an artificial nectar will bring in hummingbirds when the flower supply is inadequate. Hummingbirds are such colorful and fascinating creatures, and such fun to watch buzzing around a garden, that many people put out sweet artificial solutions to enhance their chance of having hummers in their yard. Packages of dry nectarlike preparation are available commercially. Check the contents to be sure they are worth their price. You can prepare your own solution by combining one part ordinary table sugar boiled in four (or more) parts of water. A more nutritious solution has one part of honey in four parts of boiled water. Honey water ferments rapidly, though, and may quickly harbor a deadly fungus or other toxins. The fungus will also grow in sugar water, but not as easily. No matter what type of solution you use, the only way to feed hummingbirds safely is to change the contents of the feeders frequently and clean them often, boiling them if possible.

Hummingbird feeders come in a variety of styles, but all are basically a container to hold a supply of sweet liquid that will flow slowly out through a tube or into a basin with a tiny hole in its cover when a hummingbird inserts its tongue and sucks. A perch is not necessary because hummingbirds can hover to feed, but they will use a perch if one is provided. Multiple feeding ports or tubes may be useful in the western states where many species of hummingbirds live and where they are perhaps less aggressive with each other. The East has only one breeding species, the Ruby-throated Hummingbird, which is notoriously feisty and territorial. If you want to see more than one hummer in your eastern yard, you'll need some luck. Normally a single bird will defend its feeder against all comers, even its mate!

Because hummingbirds are attracted by red in flowers, most feeders are red where the liquid comes out. A few drops of red food coloring added to the liquid itself will also make it more visible and attractive—at least until your local hummers have found the feeder.

Orioles have something of a sweet tooth that they normally satisfy with fruit. But they do love nectar, too, and your solution will attract any in the area, winter or summer. Orioles can't hover as the hummers do, though, and they are considerably larger birds. In order to afford them access to your nectar, you would need to use a large feeder with perches or you could use a *shallow* dish or saucer.

Pest problems with hummingbird feeders can be frustrating. Ants and bees are fond of sugar and are difficult to exclude. Most bee guards on commercially made feeders don't work, probably because the sweet liquid drips from the tube after the bird has left or is spilled by the hummer itself, or because the bees are able to reach

Top: *Orioles are just as fond of sugar water as hummingbirds are, and you may find one trying to take a turn at your feeder.* Above: *A group of hummingbirds share a feeder together. This type of feeder has a perch, which some of the hummers are using, and an ant guard.*

A hummer sips nectar from a flower.

past the guard into the reservoir of liquid. Carefully check the design of a feeder before buying it to see whether you think bees can be kept out of it. Ants are so small and agile that they are almost impossible to exclude from a nectar feeder, or anywhere else for that matter. Unfortunately, the only practical answers for ants are to treat any possible access routes to the feeder with an insecticide or to use a barrier, such as a pool of salad oil, that ants can't get past. You have to use extreme care here, though. These measures pose a potential threat to your birds and to the rest of your immediate environment. If you use an insecticide, take the time to find one that is ecologically safe, and be sure that you always store and dispense these materials responsibly. If ants have found their way into a hanging feeder, your best bet is to wrap some heavy-duty tape — sticky side up — around their access to the wire or to purchase a commercially available ant guard. The ant guard is a small cup that fits around the wire and holds salad oil or some other barrier.

Hummers hovering gracefully as they sip from your feeder make a unique and rewarding sight.

CHAPTER 3

Attracting Birds with Water

Offering food is an excellent strategy for attracting birds to your yard, but there's something that will act as an even bigger draw: water. You would never be able to offer foods that are attractive to every type of bird in your region, but they *all* need water for drinking and bathing no matter what their eating preferences are. An obvious and abundant supply of water will make your yard a potential stopping place for virtually every bird in the general area.

If you are lucky enough to have a brook or pond in or near your yard, you can make it even more appealing to birds by creating drinking and bathing pools. Choose a spot where your view of the birds will be unimpeded and where predators cannot hide, and then clear away the grass, weeds, or other vegetation on the shore. Spread some sand or gravel on either side of the water's edge to make a small beach for landing and a shallow spot two or three inches deep for drinking and bathing. You might also try positioning three or four large rocks in the water so that their tops are just below the surface.

Most yards have no natural water, though, so you will have to provide a birdbath or artificial pond. For water to be acceptable to a bird, it should be clean, no deeper than about two and a half inches, and preferably with a sloping bottom so that very small birds can visit the shallower edges. A birdbath should have a rough bottom for good footholds and it should be well out in the open, away from any hiding places for predators. A birdbath well above ground is safest; when birds really get into their enthusiastic dunking and fluttering, they may forget to keep a lookout for danger. Perching places should also be nearby because a wet bird is vulnerable—it cannot fly well with sodden feathers and needs somewhere safe to shake itself dry, preen, and regain its ability to take off quickly.

It's up to you to decide what kind and size of birdbath you want, but it's simpler to keep one large bath clean and full than several smaller ones, and birds don't seem to mind sharing with their neighbors. The simplest kind of birdbath can be made by setting a large flowerpot saucer securely on a stump or on the ground. A garbage can lid upside down on the ground also makes a good cheap birdbath, but beware of one that might be too deep or that has hard-to-clean crevices.

The easiest, most common birdbath is a cement or terra-cotta basin on a pedestal, the kind usually found in garden centers or hardware stores. This type is often attractive and probably safest for a cat-filled neighborhood, but it is breakable, and it may crack in freezing weather unless it is emptied.

A Florida Scrub Jay perches atop an outdoor spigot. Birds have a need for water, of course, but they also seem to have a great love for it. They will be drawn to almost any source of water, and it's one of the most effective lures you can offer.

In their urban environments, Rock Doves can find ready sources of water everywhere.

If you are a serious landscaper and your yard is the showplace of the neighborhood, you might want to get creative with a birdbath, making an artistic pedestal or a grotto of wood or natural stone to hold the basin. Or you could make an artificial pond, with shallow areas for the birds and deeper sections for fish.

If you really want to get fancy, as well as making your birdbath especially attractive to birds, consider providing them with water that *moves*. Why are birds drawn to moving water? Why do we humans like babbling brooks, rushing streams, waterfalls, fountains, even shower baths? It's probably the same answer for both of us, but fortunately the birds aren't as particular as we are. They will be just as drawn to a garbage can lid on the ground with a pail suspended over it, dripping water down a nail stuck through a very small hole in the bottom, as they are to an expensive fine-spray fountain set up over an elaborate stone birdbath.

One of the more pleasant features of a birdbath is that you'll often see widely different species sharing it.

Perhaps the most convenient way to provide moving water is to buy a special small hose fitting, available at many garden centers or by specialty mail order; attach a long, narrow length of tubing to the spigot, suspend the other end over the birdbath or pond, and adjust the water flow to a slow drip. You won't waste water that way, and the task of cleaning and filling the birdbath will be cut to a minimum.

A bird fountain can be very attractive, but it's not necessarily the best choice. Most fountains recirculate their water, so keeping the basin clean and filled is as much work as in a common birdbath. And many fountains have lead components, which are deadly poisonous to almost any form of life. Perhaps it would be simpler to turn on your lawn sprinkler and let the birds enjoy that from time to time.

Whatever method you choose, the sight and sound of moving water will increase the number of bird visits, especially by migrating birds that pass through the area and don't know the water is there.

As with feeders, birdbaths should be easy to keep clean, whether they are plain or fancy. Although algae build up quickly in summer, a stiff brush will usually do the job nicely, even on a rough concrete

Top: *A Rock Dove bends its head for a drink.*
Above: *Two Mourning Doves make use of a backyard bath. This could be a mating pair, and the ready source of water may encourage them to choose a nest site in the immediate vicinity.*

bath. If the problem becomes a serious nuisance, scrub the bath well with a chlorinated cleanser and rinse thoroughly before refilling. But you will soon realize that a well-used birdbath, like your own bathtub, gets dirty quickly and needs attention often. It's not well known, but some species of birds will even use a birdbath to wash their food before eating it, and you may find evidence of that when you scrub out the basin. A bath does require some effort on your part — there's no getting around that — but it can be quite rewarding to know you're providing your birds with something they really need and enjoy.

There is some controversy about the advisability of providing heated water for birds in winter. The main objection is that the birds will bathe in it as well as drink it. Their feathers, however, are such that when birds bathe, the outer feathers become wet but the inner downy fluff stays dry and keeps the water away from the skin. Therefore, most birds should not be harmed by being chilled after a winter bath.

Birdbath heaters have become common on the market, and they probably do more good than harm. Your own experience and the severity of your area's winters will help you decide if you need one. Although birds must have drinking water regardless of the temperature outside, for centuries they have gotten along just fine by using snow. However, if water is not naturally available in a form that birds can use, you should provide it. This can be done in a couple of ways.

On mornings when the temperature is below freezing, you can fill a flat pan with hot water and set it on the ground; the warmth in the soil should help the water stay liquid most of the day. If your winter temperatures are such that water freezes quickly and stays that way all day, you may want to invest in a commercial birdbath immersion heater. Check to see how deep the water must be to cover the heater. If your regular birdbath is too shallow, use a deeper substitute for the duration. You can also set some bricks or large stones in the new basin that will help hold the heater in place and give the birds a rough surface in shallow water to perch on.

A couple of cautions about water in winter. First, some people will set up a light bulb in their birdbaths in order to heat the water; the heat generated by the bulb keeps water liquid in all but the most extreme temperatures. This is *not* recommended, however. Rigging this kind of setup involves water and electricity, and your efforts could easily result in a serious hazard to the birds or to yourself. Also, never add glycerine or antifreeze to your birdbath to keep the water liquid. These substances are toxic, and they can destroy the vital waterproofing ability of a bird's feathers. You'll almost certainly end up killing birds this way. Another thing to keep in mind is that ceramic basins may crack from temperature stresses created by water and cold weather. You may want to find a less aesthetic but more practical substitute for the colder months, such as a garbage can lid.

A robin shows that birds not only like to drink water, they also like to splash around in it.

Water movement, even if it's just a slow, steady drip, makes water much more noticeable to birds.

Birds can find water even in the dead of winter, as this tiny junco demonstrates.

Attracting Birds with Nest Boxes

A bluebird firmly stakes its claim to this nest box. Not many varieties of bird will accept a nest box, but many of the ones that do are lively and interesting species. It's also an excellent way to entice them into your yard.

Hundreds upon hundreds of bird species nest in the United States, but only about 85 use cavities, and some of these insist on finding or digging their own. More than 50, however, will gladly accept a nest box (bird house) if you put up the kind they want and if you put it in a suitable place. The trick is in finding out what they want and where they want it.

Almost any region will have two or three local hole-nesters. Some other birds will accept a nest shelf, and still others will use materials you provide to construct their own nest. The birds will welcome the help, for natural sites such as dead trees are rare in most residential areas.

Don't make the mistake of rushing out and buying the first bird house that catches your eye. First, learn which of your local species will nest in a box and decide which you want to offer accommodations for. That will determine what size the box and its hole should be, how high the hole should be from the box floor, and what sort of location would be most suitable. *Then* shop for, or make, the specific sort of nest box that will suit the birds you want to attract. If you don't do this, the generalized bird house you buy may be totally ignored, except by wasps or mice.

A nest box, whether homemade or store-bought, should have certain qualities. It should be made of sturdy, weatherproof materials, preferably wood—not metal, which will heat up and bake the nestlings on a hot day—with brass or galvanized hardware so that it will last for several years. The box should have several ½-inch holes for drainage and ventilation, and it should also be easy to clean. There are many good boxes on the market, but if you are even marginally handy with a saw and hammer, it's simple, less expensive, and enjoyable to spend a weekend or two making your own.

Select well-seasoned, durable wood such as ¾-inch redwood, cypress, or cedar, and hardware that will not rust—otherwise the boards will eventually loosen and let moisture in. After deciding which species' box you will build, sketch on paper the best way to cut the various pieces; many of the recommended dimensions are such that you can buy a board of the appropriate width and cut the box pieces with a minimum of work and waste. Before assembling the box, drill three or four ½-inch drainage holes in the floor piece and another three holes near the top of each of the side pieces for ventilation. Then drill the correct size of entrance hole, remembering that a too-small hole will exclude the bird you want, but a larger hole may permit undesired birds like House Sparrows or European Starlings to squeeze in instead. Nail or screw the sides and front so

Nest boxes can have the same basic design, but they must fit the species they're meant for. This House Wren requires one of the smallest boxes.

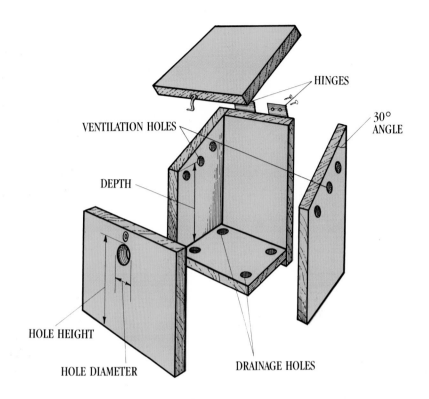

NEST BOX DIMENSIONS

Species	Floor (inches)	Depth (inches)	Hole Height (inches)	Hole Diameter (inches)	Mounting Height (feet)
American Kestrel	8×8	12-15	9-12	3	10-40
Screech-owl	8×8	12-15	9-12	3	10-30
Saw-whet Owl	6×6	10-12	8-10	2½	12-20
Barn Owl	10×18	15-18	4	6	12-18
Northern Flicker	7×7	16-18	14-16	2½	6-20
Downy Woodpecker	4×4	8-10	6-8	1¼	6-20
Hairy Woodpecker	6×6	12-15	9-12	1½	12-20
Red-headed Woodpecker	6×6	12-15	9-12	2	12-20
Great Crested Flycatcher	6×6	8-10	6-8	2	8-20
Tree Swallows	5×5	6	1-5	1½	10-15
Purple Martin*	6×6	6	1	2½	15-20
Black-capped Chickadee	4×4	8-10	6-8	1⅛	6-15
Tufted Titmouse	4×4	8-10	6-8	1¼	6-15
White-breasted Nuthatch	4×4	8-10	6-8	1¼	12-20
House and Bewick's Wrens	4×4	6-8	4-6	1-1¼	6-10
Carolina Wren	4×4	6-8	4-6	1½	6-10
Eastern Bluebird	5×5	8	6	1½	5-10
House Finch	6×6	6	4	2	8-12

* Dimensions are for a single unit of a multiunit structure.

A female bluebird sits outside her nest box with a grasshopper in her beak.

they extend below the floor, to prevent water from seeping in. The roof should be hinged at the back, and it should cover the outside edges of the back and sides and extend well over the front to weatherproof and provide shade. A few small strips of wood tacked below the hole on the *inside* will help the adults get in and out before the nest is built and will help the older young to get up to the hole to be fed. That cute little perch found on the outside of so many commercial nest boxes is not only unnecessary for most hole-dwelling birds, it also makes a handy pawhold for predators. If you are worried that birds cannot easily cling to the smooth, hard surface of your box after it is painted, use a rough file on the area beneath the hole before the first coat.

If you use redwood, cypress, or cedar for the box, you can leave it to weather to a lovely natural color. If you use a cheaper wood, the box will need a protective coat or two of a good outdoor paint or stain. Wait to mount the roof piece until you've finished painting and don't use a bright color, no matter how much paint you may have left over from another job. Keep to browns, grays, or greens; birds accept earthy, natural colors much more readily. Try a

Robins will not accept nest boxes, but they will gladly use a nesting shelf to raise their brood.

mixture of paint with some oil stain and a lot of linseed oil, lightly stirred and generously spread inside and out in several coats until the wood is saturated. You'll get a durable box that will look camouflaged when it is hung in place.

After the paint or stain is thoroughly dry, mount the roof with brass hinges at the back. If brass is too expensive, you may use strips of tough leather instead, but they will need to be checked and replaced if they begin to deteriorate. One or two brass hook-and-eye fasteners will hold down the front of the roof securely and still allow easy access for cleaning.

There is little need to decorate a nest box, but if you want to make it more pleasing to the human eye, then go right ahead. Always remember, though, that birds prefer natural things. You might try covering the outside with strips of tree bark. You can also place a few twigs, wood chips, or other starter materials in the box to encourage its acceptance.

The most difficult part of providing successful nest boxes is deciding where to mount them. The site must be where the bird feels comfortable, not necessarily where you can see it from the kitchen window. Some species, especially chickadees, titmice, nuthatches, and woodpeckers, like to nest in dense shaded woods with the box on a dead stump or standing tree. Most other birds prefer to be fairly out in the open. Wrens, swallows, and bluebirds want a relatively low box, mounted about 10 feet above the ground on a post at the edge of a lawn or open field. Most other species want to be fairly high up near the edge of woods or in a grove of trees with the box in full or partial sun. If the hole is not directly in line with prevailing southerly spring winds, the box should preferably face south. The area around the front of the box must be clear of branches and other obstructions so that the incoming bird will have a clear flight path.

Some people like to put out several nest boxes. This can be done successfully, but you've got to follow a few more common-sense rules. If you make several boxes for the same species, spread them as far as possible from each other; most nesting birds demand their space. If you really get carried away with building boxes, you will be better off making a box or two for each of several different local species. A House Wren will put up with a neighboring House Finch, but not another wren. He'll just go around and fill up all the other boxes with sticks and leave you to wonder which one has the active nest in it!

Boxes seem to be most successful if they are put up the previous fall, which gives them a few months to weather, lose that new look, and become more natural. This also gives the resident birds time to explore them. Some boxes may quickly be used for roosting in cold weather. But if your box isn't ready until early spring, don't worry; put it up as soon as you can and it will still have a chance of attracting a tenant that year.

Thrashers are not cavity nesters, but they will settle in your yard if it has dense shrubs or thick undergrowth.

A group of Carolina Chickadee nestlings crowd together in a nest box as they await food.

As the nesting season progresses, some of your boxes may remain unoccupied. Try moving them to other spots. Sometimes birds, especially wrens, can be exasperating in the way they ignore the attractive little house you made for them and build instead in an old coffee can in the garage. Be patient, put the house near the preferred site, and try again. Check inside unsuccessful boxes; wasps or other undesirables may have set up housekeeping before the birds had a chance. If you suspect that predators are a problem, see Chapter 6 for suggestions about excluding pests.

After young birds have flown from a successful box, clean it out. The box may be used again that year, but not unless *you* clean it. The old nest may seem perfectly reusable, but you probably won't notice the insects or their eggs that will parasitize the next brood if left undisturbed.

One caution: When you see a pair of birds starting to show interest in a nest box, don't interfere and *don't peek*. Control your curiosity and leave them alone. If you don't, they'll almost surely abandon the box, and possibly your yard, because birds are particularly nervous during that stage of the breeding cycle. Later in the season, you may get a chance to be more closely involved with the young. If the young first flutter out of a nest and can't fly well enough to escape predators, it's all right to take a fledgling off the ground and set it in a safe bush — not back in the nest because it will just jump out again. Unlike mammals, most birds have no sense of smell and won't abandon a baby because it's been picked up by a human. From the safety of the bush, the hungry young one will soon call and let its parents know where to come and feed it.

Purple Martins are the major exceptions to rules about nest boxes. These large swallows have a deserved if somewhat exaggerated reputation for eating mosquitoes. They are also delightful to watch fluttering busily around their attractive large apartment house, uttering their curiously throaty calls. Some people think that having a colony of martins is the ultimate success in bird housing, but martins require a very specific habitat. If you live next to a lake or bay, or on the edge of a large open field, and if there are other colonies of martins in the area, you may want to try. If your carpentry skills allow, building your own house with 6-inch-square compartments and excellent ventilation will save considerable expense. The commercial models can cost $100 or more, depending on size and materials. Martins will also gladly accept a cluster of large gourds, each with a 2½-inch entrance hole (and small drainage holes in the bottom) hung from a 15-20 foot pole or strung on a high wire. Housing martins may be a lot of effort, but if you are successful, you will have endless summer entertainment as well as a relatively mosquito-free yard.

Although they are not cavity nesters, species like robins, phoebes, and Barn Swallows will accept a nesting shelf if their usual nesting sites are in short supply. Or perhaps you want to offer a shelf site that is convenient for you, either to have the nesting where it's easier to watch or to move the bird from someplace that's a nuisance. Nesting shelves are easily made with a 7-inch-square

Like many species, the bluebird (top) *and robin* (middle) *will build their own nests in your yard if conditions are suitable for them; provide nesting materials in order to encourage them. Above: You can put a perch on your nest box if you like, but there's really no need for one.*

floor (again, with drain holes), a low ledge to help keep the nest in place, and a sloping roof, much like that on a nest box. Inside a shed, garage, or barn, a simple wooden shelf, perhaps sloped slightly toward the back, will do nicely. If the shelf is inside a closed structure, though, you must be sure to leave a door, window, or some other access way open at all times. Nesting shelves are also available commercially.

Besides putting up boxes and shelves, you can also help birds in other ways during the breeding season. Many species will gladly use nest materials you offer. Hang out a mesh bag with bits of string, yarn, rags, the combings from a dog's brush — almost anything soft will rapidly disappear into the basic construction or lining of a nest. Just be sure that all such materials are less than six inches long to keep the birds from possibly becoming entangled. Birds get along pretty well on their own, but during the nesting season they will accept a surprising variety of aids.

Purple Martins will accept these hollowed gourds as eagerly as they will a manufactured nest box.

CHAPTER 5

Attracting Birds with Plants

Birds depend on plants for food, shelter, and nesting places. With planning and a modest effort, your backyard can offer all three to a much greater extent than it probably does now. As you acquire plants and work in your garden, think about the needs of the birds you are trying to attract, and adapt some of your plans accordingly. When buying a new plant, consider whether it will offer any of the three necessities of food, shelter, and nesting sites; if not, consider another type that will be equally attractive to you, but even more so to a bird. In deciding where to put the new acquisition, think also about increasing the shelter in your yard; create places where birds can hide from danger and bad weather and where the vegetation will be dense and safe for a nest. Evenly spaced plantings all in a row may satisfy a person's sense of order, but clumped bushes can be equally eye-pleasing and much more useful to your birds.

Ideally, when a yard is being enhanced for its birdlife, a detailed plan should be made. The plan should include the plants to be used and how they can best be arranged in the space available. Keep in mind how they will look to you and what the foliage, flowers, and fruits will offer to birds each season. If you are beginning with a new house that has no landscaping, you can aim for perfection right from the start. Usually, though, your yard or garden is already established, and the only practical approach is to plan a gradual change as time, energy, and finances permit.

The first basic decision to make concerns how much of the yard you want to have civilized — with mowed lawn and formal flower beds — and how much can be left natural. Neighbors might have unkind thoughts about lazy homeowners as the wild trees, shrubs, and weeds grow up, but the birds will compensate as they flock to a habitat they prefer. Having a natural landscape can also be fun for an avid gardener, as interesting new native plants are searched out from the surrounding countryside and added to what is already growing in the yard. Many towns also have nurseries that specialize in native plants to further expand your "non-garden." Even if you decide against having a wild part of your yard, keep native plants in mind when you plan for the birds because they often grow a great deal better than horticultural varieties do.

Right: An ideal backyard for birds requires effort, time, and money. Success lies in variety, and designing a yard can be quite enjoyable. Opposite page: Birds prefer a loosely ordered, natural habitat, which can also please the human eye.

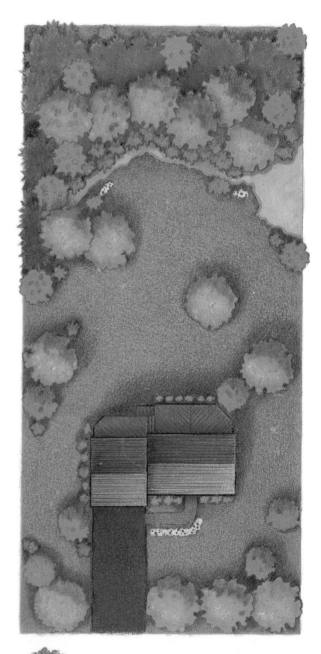

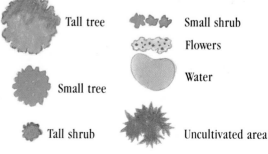

Tall tree

Small tree

Tall shrub

Small shrub

Flowers

Water

Uncultivated area

Wild cherry tree

Small trees like this crab apple are low maintenance, permanent, and very attractive to your birds.

Above: *Crab apples retain their nutritious fruit throughout the winter, offering a valuable source of food.* Left: *Larger trees such as this oak provide some nourishment and are very appealing to tree-nesting species.*

Top: *Seed-bearing parts of several evergreen trees.*
Above: *Fruiting shrubs and trees will serve different birds in a number of different ways. This towhee has no interest in the loquat fruit it's perched by; the bird is probably searching out insects that feed on the small fruit.*

When planning a landscape for birds, fruit-bearing shrubs and trees probably come to mind first. These are important, but there are many other things that birds look for. Dense evergreens are useful for winter shelter and are often used for the first nest of the season before the deciduous species leaf out. And don't forget the dense evergreen that normally gets thrown away after Christmas; it makes good shelter for a few months as part of a brush pile that can be tucked away in the back of even the tidiest garden.

The climates and soil types required for most plants to thrive are very specific. Each region of the country supports a distinctive flora, and it's difficult to make anything but general recommendations about what plants will work in your yard to attract birds. The following list contains groups of plants, *some* members of which will grow in many parts of the country. Use this list as a close guide, but develop your own unique design that suits your needs and your region. Keep in mind the basic needs of your birds — food, shelter, and nesting areas. Remember, too, that variety in what you provide equals variety in the species that come to your yard, and that your plants should be good providers in fall and winter as well as in spring and summer. Consult your local nursery or a regional garden guide for more help in selecting plants that suit your birds and grow well in your area.

TREES

A great many trees offer abundant food for birds as well as attractive tall plantings for a yard. Once planted, they can be used by birds for years without further work or expense on your part. Consider American elm (if Dutch elm disease hasn't eliminated this majestic species from your area), pines, oaks, maples, and hackberry. Smaller but usually faster-growing trees are also useful to birds, and there are a great many choices. Birches and alders provide seed in winter and are favored by chickadees, redpolls, and other small finches. Wild or cultivated cherries, crab apples, and hawthorns are great favorites of fruit-eating birds such as thrushes and mockingbirds, catbirds, and thrashers. Crab apple trees and others that hold their fruit all winter are particularly valuable; they offer both fruit and insect food — the bugs that are overwintering in the fruit provide a welcome source of protein. American holly, with its glossy evergreen foliage, is beautiful and bountiful both summer and winter. The broad variety of dogwood species, both trees and shrubs, can be a very important source of summer and winter fruit. Mountain ash has abundant red berries that are particular favorites of waxwings. Mulberries are an important source of summer fruit, but plant the tree where the fallen fruit (and the birds) don't make a mess of a driveway or patio. Red cedar is particularly choice because of its fruit; however all cedars provide excellent shelter.

Left to right: *Laurustinas, viburnum, and barberry*

SHRUBS

Heavily flowering and fruiting shrubs are the cornerstones of any yard designed for birds because they are so important for nesting places and cover as well as for the food they provide. Autumn olive is highly popular because of its abundant red berries that will hold into winter. Barberry, bayberry, buffalo berry, elderberry, multiflora rose, pyracantha, and snowberry, as well as the several varieties of shrub dogwoods and hollies, blackberries, blueberries, raspberries, cotoneasters, sumacs, and viburnums offer a huge range of choices. If hummingbirds are in your yard, don't forget the nectar-producing shrubs, like butterfly bush, beauty bush, mimosa, and weigela.

VINES

Most vines will quickly form a dense tangle that offers superb cover for nesting. Many of the honeysuckles add a bonus with their lovely scent and are great favorites of hummingbirds; the berry-producing varieties (especially Tartarian honeysuckle) are appreciated by fruit-eaters, as well. Trumpet vines and scarlet runner bean are other hummingbird favorites. Virginia creeper and wild grape also produce valuable fruit that lasts all winter.

ANNUALS AND PERENNIALS

The obvious first choice here is sunflower. A good-sized patch of the large-seed domestic varieties or of wild sunflower will save somewhat on your winter seed bill, and it's fun to watch the birds as they dig the seed from the heavy heads in winter. You may also want to try planting other bird seeds, like white millet, instead of buying the entire winter's supply. Decorative annuals produce seed that birds like too; let your marigolds, zinnias, and phlox go to seed and small finches will work on the heads through the winter. Hummingbirds much prefer the flowers in your garden over the sugar water in the feeder, so plant a variety of flowers for nectar, preferably those that are tube-shaped and red: bee balm (*Monarda*) and cardinal flower (*Lobelia*) are special favorites, but begonia, columbine, daylily, delphinium, foxglove, fuchsia, geranium, gladiolus, hollyhock, lupine, morning glory, nicotiana, petunia, phlox, pink, sage, scabiosa, shrimp plant, snapdragon, and spider plant are all attractive to hummingbirds.

And don't forget the weeds. A lot of the plants that just appear in gardens grew from seeds dropped by birds. If an untidy look doesn't bother you too much, leave the volunteers to grow and produce another crop of bird food: pokeberries, sumac, elderberries, dogwoods, wild cherries and plums, honeysuckle, and red cedar are just some of the species that birds distribute themselves.

Top: *Sunflowers are an excellent natural source of seed.* Above: *This varied planting of foxglove, peonies, and other flowers will appeal to birds that like nectar, seed, or dense undergrowth.*

Weigela

A tanager perches in a wild, grassy meadow.

A Scrub Jay finds a source of winter fruit.

This robin has food and a possible nest site.

CHAPTER 6

Common Problems and What To Do About Them

Where can I buy the products I need?

At one time, most feeders and nest boxes had to be made at home because very few suitable ones were manufactured for sale. Fortunately, a wide variety of excellent products has now become available, as interest in the hobby has grown. If you are not handy with tools or have limited time to spend, almost anything you need is commercially available in a wide price range. Most discount stores carry a small selection of inexpensive items, usually made of plastic; some are excellent. They may break easily or they may have no resilience against an impatient squirrel, but they are cheap to replace. Sturdier equipment and higher quality seed are usually found at local nature centers and stores that sell garden supplies, agricultural feed, or hardware. Top-of-the-line and specialty products are available by mail order from companies that sell bird-related products exclusively. The following are some that offer catalogs:

Audubon Workshop, 1501 Paddock Dr., Northbrook, IL 60062
BackYard Birds & Co., 717 S. Broadway, Springfield, MO 65809
The Crow's Nest Birding Shop, Cornell Laboratory of
    Ornithology, 159 Sapsucker Woods Road, Ithaca, NY 14850
Duncraft, Penacook, NH 03303

What can be done when a bird nest causes a problem?

Some species commonly place their nests inside buildings when there is free access, so you may find yourself having to leave a garage door open for a bird that set up housekeeping and now needs to fly in and out every few minutes to feed the babies. Carolina Wrens are notorious for building nests with lightning speed in the oddest places — like the pocket of a shirt hung out to dry. Birds using human structures as nest sites, however, seldom cause a serious problem. The most common one is probably when the excrement falling from a nest makes too much of a mess (especially true of Barn Swallows). If you do want to get rid of a nest, the best way is simply to block access to the nest site and provide an alternative spot nearby. Most birds will take the hint and oblige you.

If you are fortunate enough to have a colony of Chimney Swifts breed in your chimney, you may worry that the tiny stick nests glued to the inside of the flue pose a fire hazard. If it's a large colony, check to see how many nests, and thus how many flammable sticks, are in there before you use the fireplace for the first time the following winter. There's seldom a serious problem unless the colony is many years old and the fireplace hasn't been used for a long time.

Equipment is available from many sources, but mail-order companies offer the widest selection.

Barn Swallows are just one of many species that are comfortable nesting inside buildings.

Can I harm birds by feeding them?

Throughout this book, the importance of keeping feeders, birdbaths, and nest boxes clean has been emphasized. By nature, birds will avoid spoiled food, dirty water, and pest-infested nest boxes; but under extreme conditions they may not be able to do so — necessity drives them to it. As long as you're careful about sanitation, you'll have no adverse affects on the birds you feed. The only "unnatural" thing you are doing is increasing the number of birds that would normally occur in one place. Don't worry that your feeders or nest boxes will affect birds' natural behavior. When it comes time for the migratory species to move on, they will go regardless of how much bountiful food is still available.

Why do birds crash into my windows, and how can I avoid it?

Birds fly into windows, often killing themselves, because they can't see the invisible barrier. Usually "killer" windows create the illusion of a clear flight path, as when there are windows opposite each other in a room. Other killer windows act as mirrors, throwing a reflection of the sky or the surrounding landscape. The best way to remove the danger is to eliminate the illusion by keeping the curtain closed. If that is not possible, try putting a hawk or owl silhouette on the glass; birds will seldom fly toward a predator. Silhouettes are commercially available, or you can paint your own, using very large eyes for the owls. For a temporary solution, smear the outside of the window lightly with opaque dish washing detergent; the soap cuts down on the mirror affect and can be hosed off later. A permanent solution is to hang strands of monofilament nylon from the outside edge of the roof over the window and weight or tie the strand bottoms. A bird flying toward the window at breakneck speed will hit the line first and slow down enough that its crash into the window will not be fatal. And the thin nylon line should not seriously interfere with your view out the window.

How can I discourage feeder pests?

Feeders attract all sorts of birds and animals, some of which become pests because they eat so much. There are ways to discourage particular nuisances, but you will save yourself irritation if you accept that food on the ground is fair game for anything. Decoy areas, with cheap items (bread, corn) well away from the "good-bird" feeders near the house will often satisfy the pests and they will leave the other feeders alone. Rock Doves (pigeons) have such large bodies that they cannot fit onto small feeders or get through large wire mesh. Use feeders with narrow perches or cover

Most birds will recognize this image as a threat and will avoid the window even if it appears to offer a clear flight path.

them with chicken wire. European Starlings and House Sparrows will usually avoid feeders very near a house or on a windowsill. Starlings also seldom feed very early in the morning or very late in the afternoon, so food put out then is often cleaned up by other birds before the starlings arrive. Do not use bread or kitchen scraps as feed unless you are willing to have starlings. House Sparrows are less of a problem because they seldom occur in large numbers, but they are also hard to avoid because they are small in body size and like the same kinds of seeds as the preferred species do. Perhaps you can put up with the sparrows and starlings in winter, if you will just think about the many insects they eat in summer.

Squirrels are so incredibly resourceful that part of the fun of feeding birds lies in trying to outwit them. Hang feeders on wires out of jumping range from the ground (about 6 feet) and from the nearest trees or buildings (8 feet). Or mount feeders with a domed, conical, or plate-like guard that squirrels cannot climb around. Or hang feeders from wires strung with sections of loose, slippery tubing alternating with old phonograph records. The tubes make it difficult to keep a foothold, and the records will tip under the animal's weight and dump it to the ground. Commercially made counter-weighted feeders only work if they are made entirely of chew-proof metal; good ones are expensive.

How can I predator-proof a nest box?

Don't use outside perches on nest boxes; the birds don't need them, but predators find them very handy. A metal sleeve, about 30 inches wide, wrapped around and then tacked to the post you use for a nest box should keep cats, raccoons, snakes, and other predators from reaching the box. If the box is mounted on a tree, you may want to use two sleeves, above and below. Whatever other type of device, such as a metal cone, you have found effective in keeping squirrels out of your feeder will also work on nest boxes, but make the guards larger because you are dealing with larger animals. Squirrels can also be nest box problems because they eat eggs and baby birds, and they can chew their way into most bird houses. Protect against squirrel depredations by nailing a metal ring or pieces of sheet metal around the entrance hole, but be sure not to leave sharp edges that will injure the birds. Dulling bright metal with dark paint is always a good idea.

I have limited space; how can I attract birds to a small patio or balcony?

The principle is essentially the same as starting from a backyard. Try scattering bits of white bread to see which species are in the neighborhood and are bold enough to come to this magnet food. Most birds are particularly hesitant about feeding on high balconies. Your success will depend in part on how easy it is for them to find food in safer places, but usually there are some brave souls around. Once you've drawn a clientele, switch to a feeder supplied with what they like. You may find that birds do not want to come in to feed, but if water is scarce, they'll almost surely be glad to use that. Start with a large flat pan with a rough bottom, and then consider a better birdbath as the birds become steady visitors.

This setup offers two obstacles to pests: The baffle blocks access to the feeder and the metal bands and small seed holes block access to the food.

Bird Profiles

Northern Oriole

F or many people, the real pleasure of having birds in their yards is the simple enjoyment of the songs, the colors, and the ceaseless activity. For others, the hobby is a more studious thing; they keep detailed journals of their visitors' daily routines and their feeding, courtship, and nesting behaviors. Wherever your interest in birds lies, successfully attracting them requires some knowledge of the different species' habits and preferences. The profiles that follow offer an interesting and useful introduction to the natural history of many of North America's most common backyard birds.

Each profile includes several species that are representative of a particular bird group. Generally, the profiles are arranged scientifically by family, with the most primitive groups coming first and the more evolved species last. In one or two instances, though, groups include birds that share common behaviors or lifestyles but belong to different families; these exceptions are noted in the introduction to each profile. For each profiled species, you'll find information on its range in North America, natural diet, usual habitat, and nesting behaviors. You'll also learn how to identify these birds and, most importantly, what you can do to attract them to your yard.

In time, your interest in your backyard birds and your expertise at observing them will grow. The common birds found in your area and their regular habits will become familiar sights. You may want to learn more about your regular visitors, and you may want to identify the species that only show up on occasion. For a more thorough and complete reference source, turn to a regional field guide of birds.

House Finch

Blue Jay

BIRDS OF PREY

American Kestrel (*Falco sparverius*),
Eastern Screech-owl (*Otus asio*),
Western Screech-owl (*Otus kennicottii*), and **Barn Owl** (*Tyto alba*)

Large carnivorous birds such as hawks, falcons, eagles, and owls are often referred to as "raptors," a convenient name that groups them together by food habits and behavior even though they are not all related. Some people are uncomfortable about having such dedicated hunters in their yards, but if that doesn't bother you, you'll find these creatures to be graceful and fascinating. These four relatively small raptor species are commonly found around houses or farms, and all will use nest boxes.

American Kestrel

DISTRIBUTION: American Kestrels are found throughout the U.S. during spring and summer; in winter, they leave the north-central states and Alaska for the warmer parts of their range. Barn Owls also occur over the entire country except Alaska and the north-central tier of states. Eastern Screech-owls live as far west as central Texas to eastern Montana; the range of the Western Screech-owl covers the rest of the western U.S. and southern Alaska.

IDENTIFICATION: The American Kestrel (formerly called Sparrow Hawk) is the smallest (9-12 inches) North American hawk — a slim, streamlined falcon with a rufous-red back and tail, and black-and-white "sideburn" head markings; the male's pointed wings are blue-gray, the female's are red-brown; the call is a rapid, shrill *killy-killy-killy.* The screech-owls are small (7-10 inches) and either gray or reddish-brown with short "ear" tufts; the two species look identical, but their calls differ — the eastern bird has a long descending whinny and a single-pitched trill, but the western has a short trill followed by a longer one (which is a duet between a male and female) or a series of accelerating hollow whistles. The Barn Owl is 14-20 inches, slim, and pale with long legs, a heart-shaped face and no ear tufts; its calls may seem frightening — loud screams and hisses.

HABITAT: You'll have the best success with these rugged loners if you live in a rural setting, or at least have large tracts of undeveloped land nearby; city dwellers shouldn't give up all hope — these birds sometimes settle in large parks and from there they may move to your yard. The kestrel lives in open country (especially with scattered trees), in farmlands and pastures, deserts, and urban and suburban areas. Screech-owls live in open woodlands, forests, old orchards, parks, and wooded residential areas. The Barn Owl is found world-wide, often near buildings, especially barns, silos, or church belfries in woodlands, farmlands, and towns.

DIET: These raptors will eat almost any live animal food that is not too large to handle: grasshoppers, beetles, and other insects, rats, mice, ground squirrels, rabbits, shrews, bats and other mammals, and the occasional small bird, snake, crawfish, frog, salamander, fish, or worm. Screech-owls have even been known to tackle a roosting pigeon when they are *really* hungry!

NESTING: Although all these raptors will use any natural cavity large enough for them — woodpecker holes in trees, crevices in cliffs — they also readily use nest boxes. The kestrel lays 3-7 eggs that are incubated for 29-30 days by the female; the young leave the nest in about 30 days. Screech-owls lay 3-8 eggs that are incubated mostly by the female for 26 days; the young fly after 28-30 days. The Barn Owl usually nests in tall buildings; it does not

use any material for its nest, but lays 5-11 eggs in the bottom of a cavity or on a rafter; the eggs are incubated by the female for 32-34 days and the young fly in 52-56 days. In most raptors, the male hunts for and feeds his mate while she is incubating the eggs.

HOW TO ATTRACT: All of these raptors will accept a nest box, and that's really the only strategy for enticing one into your yard. The kestrel likes its nest 10-20 feet above the ground on a large dead tree or pole in an open field or pasture. Screech-owls will take a nest box placed 10-13 feet above the ground on the main trunk or large vertical branch of a tree, preferably in dense woods. Owl boxes should be located well away from a house because the parents will defend their nests by attacking intruders. Screech-owls are known to visit birdbaths at night; if you don't put up a nest box, you might still draw one with your water. Barn Owls require a nest box 12-18 feet above the ground in a large tree in the open. Where Barn Owls are already nesting in a building but the site seems precarious, a 10×18-inch platform will often be accepted if nailed securely near the original nest.

Western Screech-owl

Barn Owl

Eastern Screech-owl

DOVES, QUAIL, AND PHEASANT

Mourning Dove (*Zenaida macroura*),
Inca Dove (*Columbina inca*),
Northern Bobwhite (*Colinus virginianus*), and **Ring-necked Pheasant** (*Phasianus colchicus*)

The doves are not related to the quail and pheasant, but they have some similar habits, especially their preferred foods and the way they flock in to feed on the ground. The doves are much smaller than the other birds, they are more common, and they are more aerial; quail and pheasant prefer the ground to the air, and they usually only fly when danger demands it of them.

Mourning Doves

Inca Dove

DISTRIBUTION: During spring and summer, Mourning Doves are found throughout the U.S. except Alaska; in fall, they migrate from the north-central states for more southern wintering grounds. Inca Doves occur only in the Southwest, from Texas to California. Northern Bobwhites are eastern birds, extending to the western Great Plains except in the northernmost states; they have also been introduced in parts of the Northwest. Because they have been widely introduced as game birds, Ring-necked Pheasant have a broad but spotty distribution across the northern half of the U.S. and in parts of the Southwest.

IDENTIFICATION: The two doves are similar in appearance with slim bodies and with long white-edged tails. The Mourning Dove is 11-13 inches, brown-gray with black spots on the wing, a pink wash on the underparts, and pink feet; its call is a mournful *oo-ah, cooo-cooo-cooo*. The Inca Dove is 7½-8 inches, with grayish scalloped plumage and bright chestnut visible in the open wing; its call is a two-noted *coo-coo*. The Northern Bobwhite reaches 10½ inches and is a mottled, reddish-brown, plump quail with a short tail; the male has a white eye stripe and neck, but these areas are buffy in the female; bobwhites are named for their call, a loud whistled *bob-WHITE*. The Ring-necked Pheasant is large (30-36 inches), chickenlike, and has a long tail; the striking male has an iridescent green/purple head, a red face, and a white neck ring; the female is dull mottled brown; pheasant have a guttural *cuck-cuck* call.

HABITAT: The Mourning Dove is widespread in open woodlands, in cultivated lands with scattered trees and bushes, in suburbs, and in arid country near water. The Inca Dove is found in semiarid open country with scattered trees and shrubs near water; it also is common in cultivated areas, parks, and gardens. Bobwhites prefer brushy fields, grasslands, farmlands, and open woodlands. Pheasant like open country, farmlands (especially grain fields), hedgerows, brush fields, and open woodlands.

DIET: These birds feed almost entirely on waste grains (especially wheat and corn) and on small seeds of grasses and weeds. They will occasionally eat small fruits, insects, plant shoots, and even nuts. These species normally gather up large amounts of food, store it in their craw, and then eat it slowly after they've retired to a safer, more comfortable area.

NESTING: Mourning Doves lay 1-4 eggs that are incubated by the male during the day and by the female at night for 14-15 days; the young fly from the nest in 14-15 days and are independent in a week. Inca Doves lay 2 eggs that are incubated by both parents for about 14 days; the young fly in another 12-14 days. Bobwhites, in contrast, lay 12-20 eggs in a grass-lined, covered depression on the ground; both parents incubate the eggs for 23-24 days and the young stay with their parents, but they leave the nest almost immediately and can fly 14 days later. Pheasant lay 6-15 eggs in a grass-lined depression in the ground; incubation is for 23-25 days by the female alone; the chicks leave the nest immediately with their mother and can fly short distances in 7 days.

HOW TO ATTRACT: Doves are tame dooryard birds and come readily to the ground under feeders, eating the cracked corn, millet, milo, sunflower, and small seed spilled by other species. They also welcome birdbaths. Bobwhites are more shy but will also come to food such as white bread, sunflower seed, millet, oats, and whole or cracked corn scattered on the ground, and they will take the berries and seeds from your garden trees and shrubs; their common western relatives, California Quail (*Callipepla californica*) and Gambel's Quail (*C. gambelii*), have distinctive black topknots and also come to grains on the ground. Pheasant are usually even more timid than quail, but you can draw them out with whole or cracked corn put out on the ground, well away from the house.

Northern Bobwhites

Ring-necked Pheasant

HUMMINGBIRDS

Anna's Hummingbird

Ruby-throated Hummingbird
(*Archilochus colubris*),
Black-chinned Hummingbird
(*Archilochus alexandri*), and **Anna's Hummingbird** (*Calypte anna*)

Of all the species of hummingbirds found in the U.S., only eight occur well north of the Mexican border. Seven of these are western birds; only the Ruby-throat breeds in the East. All may occasionally be seen at garden flowers in the right habitat, but only the three discussed here are regulars in yards. Hummers can be difficult to please, and your efforts to attract them will not really bring any *other* birds to your yard, but they certainly are worth the effort. They will be among the most active and unique visitors you have, constantly flitting, buzzing, and hovering, and their courtship flights are some of the most intricate and unusual in the bird kingdom.

DISTRIBUTION: The eastern Ruby-throated Hummingbird is highly migratory, spending the breeding season from Minnesota to Texas and winter in the southernmost U.S. through Central America. The Black-chinned Hummingbird occurs from Texas west and also migrates south of the Mexican border in winter. Anna's Hummingbird lives year-round along the West Coast and as far inland as Arizona.

IDENTIFICATION: Hummingbirds are tiny, and they have fused wingbones, so the wings cannot bend or fold as in other birds. Wing movement is from the shoulder, allowing the characteristic high-tempo, insectlike flight. Hummingbirds hover in midair as well as fly up, down, forward, even backward as they visit your flowers. Ruby-throated Hummingbirds are 3-4 inches long, iridescent green above and white below with a brilliant ruby-red throat in the male; the high squeaky call note is seldom heard. The Black-chinned Hummingbird is the western counterpart of the eastern Ruby-throat; it differs by the male having a violet throat below the black chin. In both species, the throat patch will look black unless bright sunlight is shining directly on the iridescent feathers. Anna's Hummingbird is slightly larger (up to 4 inches), also metallic green above and white below, but the male is rosy red over most of the top of his head and throat, and the female usually has a few rosy feathers on her throat. Most female hummingbirds are very similar to one another and hard to tell apart.

HABITAT: Ruby-throats occur in open mixed woodlands, parks, and other areas with scattered trees; they also visit flowers in meadows and gardens. Black-chinned and Anna's hummingbirds are found in open woodlands, scrub, desert washes, chaparral, and parks and gardens, usually in arid areas.

DIET: Ruby-throats are strongly attracted to red flowers, which they visit for nectar and insects. They are often found at columbines in spring and later at scarlet sage, trumpet honeysuckle, bee balm, jewelweed, phlox, petunias, lilies, trumpet vine, and nasturtiums. They also feed on tree sap and many small insects, even those trapped in spiderwebs. Black-chins visit tree tobacco, scarlet larkspur, chuparosa, paloverdes, and other flowers for nectar. They also eat pollen and insects. Anna's Hummingbird uses flowers of eucalyptus, tree tobacco, century plant, and other plants and also feeds on tree sap. It feeds on spiders and insects more than any other North American hummingbird.

NESTING: Male hummingbirds are never involved in nesting duties. The female Ruby-throat builds a beautiful, compact little nest of plant downs felted together with spider silk or strands from a tent caterpillar nest. The nest is camouflaged with lichen and often built over a small stream or other water. When complete, it looks like a natural knot on a tree branch. The entire nest is small enough to be covered by a bottle cap. Two white eggs, the size of small beans, are incubated for 16 days; the young fly 20-22 days later. Anna's Hummingbird also builds a nest of soft plant downs and adds lichen as outer camouflage. She incubates her 2 eggs for 14-18 days, and the young leave the nest 18-21 days later. The Black-chinned Hummingbird's nest is almost identical, but lichen is not used on the outside. The 2-3 eggs are incubated for 16 days, and the young leave the nest 20 days after hatching.

HOW TO ATTRACT: All these hummingbirds will come to sugar-water feeders and flowers in gardens. For detailed suggestions on feeding hummingbirds, see Chapters 2 and 5.

Ruby-throated Hummingbird

Black-chinned Hummingbird

WOODPECKERS AND FLICKERS

Northern Flicker (*Colaptes auratus*), **Downy Woodpecker** (*Picoides pubescens*), and **Red-bellied Woodpecker** (*Melanerpes carolinus*)

Members of the woodpecker family are best known for the pounding they do on trees, fence posts, and houses. They do this primarily to search for insects and their larvae found within the wood and to excavate nest holes during breeding season. Some woodpeckers also drum loudly on especially resonant pieces of wood to announce their presence in a territory early in the breeding season.

DISTRIBUTION: Northern Flickers are found in all parts of the U.S, but they migrate out of Alaska during the winter. Downy Woodpeckers also have a huge range, inhabiting almost all regions of the country except the desert Southwest. Red-bellied Woodpeckers breed in the East from Minnesota to Texas; they leave the northernmost parts of their range during winter.

IDENTIFICATION: The Northern Flicker is a 12-14 inch brown woodpecker with a white rump patch (conspicuous in flight), a whitish breast with black spots, and a solid black "necklace." There are three different versions of this bird; they were once classified separately but are now considered to be the same species. Eastern birds (formerly the Yellow-shafted Flicker) are bright golden yellow under the wings and tail, and the male has a black "mustache" stripe. Western birds (Red-shafted Flicker) are red where the eastern flickers are yellow, and the males have a red mustache. Flickers in the southwestern deserts (Gilded Flicker) are smaller (10-12 inches), with yellow linings to the wings and tail, and a red mustache on the males. Calls are a loud, rapid *wick-a-wick-a-wick-a* or a single *klee-yer.* Downy Woodpeckers are small (6-7 inches) and entirely black-and-white except for a red patch on

Red-bellied Woodpecker

Downy Woodpecker

the back of the male's head. The Downy's call is a high, descending whinny. Red-bellied Woodpeckers are poorly named; their lower abdomen is only faintly tinged with red, and it's not a very useful way to identify them. Red-bellieds have black-and-white striped wings and backs, a white breast and face, and extensive red on the back of the head (and forehead, in males). Their call is a rolling *churr* or a cackling *kek-kek*.

HABITAT: All of the birds in this group settle in heavily treed areas, as you would expect. Flickers occur in forests, open woodlands, along waterways, and in parks and suburbs; they also frequent large cacti in deserts. Downy Woodpeckers live in deciduous or mixed forests, parks, orchards, and suburbs. Red-bellied Woodpeckers occur in open woodlands, second-growth trees, wooded swamps, parks, and towns.

DIET: All woodpeckers drill holes in trees for grubs, beetles, and other wood-boring insects and ants. Flickers also feed heavily on ants, grasshoppers, and caterpillars on the ground and on wasps and other flying insects. They eat wild fruit, dogwood berries, and some weed seeds. Downy and Red-bellied woodpeckers dig in trees and flake off tree bark as they search for insects, grubs, and eggs. They also eat caterpillars, beetles, weevils, and other insects, and some wild fruit and berries, nuts, and tree sap.

NESTING: Woodpeckers drill cavities in trees for both roosting and nesting. Both the male and female take turns excavating and, later, incubating the eggs. Flickers prefer dead stubs, digging a cavity 10-36 inches deep, with a 2-4 inch hole. They use a layer of fresh chips in the bottom as nest material on which 5-10 eggs are laid. Incubation is for 11-12 days; the young fly 25-28 days later. Downy Woodpeckers, with their smaller bodies and shorter bills, dig in smaller dead snags, but they will use a live tree if necessary. The cavity is gourd-shaped, 8-12 inches deep with a 1½ inch entrance and a few chips in the bottom. Their 3-7 eggs are incubated for 12 days, and the young leave the nest after 21-24 days. Red-bellied Woodpeckers use soft-wood trees like cottonwood, elm, basswood, and sycamore, and they prefer partly decayed stubs or limbs. They will also nest in cabbage palms, utility poles, and fence posts. The cavity is 10-12 inches deep with a 2 inch hole; 3-8 eggs are incubated for 11-12 days, and the young fly 24-26 days after hatching.

HOW TO ATTRACT: All three of these woodpeckers will visit feeders for suet, bread, and peanut butter mixtures. Downies and Red-bellieds are especially fond of such fare and will also eat doughnuts and nut meats. Flickers and Downies will accept nest boxes mounted on a dead tree or pole 6-20 feet above the ground.

Northern Flicker

FLYCATCHERS AND PHOEBES

Great Crested Flycatcher (*Myiarchus crinitus*) and **Eastern Phoebe** (*Sayornis phoebe*)

Eastern Phoebe

The huge family of 375 species of Tyrant Flycatchers (named after the aggressive kingbirds, *Tyrannus*) lives largely in Central and South America, but 35 species reach North America, and a few, including Crested Flycatchers and Phoebes, are familiar backyard or farmyard birds during the breeding season. Flycatchers commonly hunt their food by sitting quietly on a perch until they spot a flying insect, then dart out, catch it on the wing (often with a loud snap of the bill), and return to the perch to eat.

DISTRIBUTION: Great Crested Flycatchers and Eastern Phoebes occur throughout the East during breeding season, from North Dakota to Texas. In winter, Phoebes live in the southern states, but Great Crested Flycatchers will be found only in southern Florida, the majority of them having migrated to Central and South America.

IDENTIFICATION: Great Crested Flycatchers are 8-9 inches, dark olive above with a bushy crest, gray throat and breast, yellow abdomen, and a reddish tail; their call is a loud *wheep,* which people can mistake for a bird in pain. Eastern Phoebes are smaller (7 inches) but still large for their family, brownish gray above, darker gray on the head, and whitish below; the call is a distinctive *fee-be.* In the West, the closely related Say's Phoebe (*Sayornis saya*) is similar but with a cinnamon-colored wash to the underparts, and the Black Phoebe (*S. nigricans*) is strikingly black above and white below. All phoebes habitually bob their tails up and down and briefly spread them open after landing on a perch.

Great Crested Flycatcher

Great Crested Flycatcher

HABITAT: Crested Flycatchers are found in deciduous forests, open woodlands, parks, orchards, and suburbs with tall shade trees. Phoebes occur in open woodlands, areas with scattered trees, and farmlands, usually near water.

DIET: Crested Flycatchers feed on an amazing variety of insects, such as dragonflies, beetles, bees, wasps, flies, mosquitoes, grasshoppers, crickets, moths, and butterflies. Although they primarily catch flying prey, they also find insects on the ground and under crevices in tree bark, and they eat some wild fruit and berries. Phoebes specialize on beetles, wasps, flying ants, and small wild bees. They also feed on a wide variety of other insects, airborne spiders, wild fruit and berries, and even tiny fish caught in shallow water.

NESTING: Great Crested Flycatchers prefer to use a natural cavity or an old woodpecker hole. If it is over 18 inches deep, they will fill it with dead leaves and other trash before building a cup-shaped nest of twigs, leaves, and grass on top. Great Crested Flycatchers are famous for their curious habit of incorporating a cast-off snakeskin (or similarly shiny cellophane tape) in their nest; why they do it is unknown. The 4-8 eggs are incubated for 13-15 days, and the young fly 12-18 days after hatching. Eastern Phoebes nest on rock ledges and in caves, but now most commonly under bridges, under barn or shed eaves, and on rafters inside open buildings or porches. The nest is a solidly built cup of mud and moss lined with grasses, hair, and feathers, and sometimes it is built right on top of last year's nest. Incubation of the 3-8 eggs is for 14-17 days, and the young leave 15-16 days after that.

HOW TO ATTRACT: Great Crested Flycatchers will use a nest box and will also feed on wild cherries, dogwood berries, mulberries, and virginia creeper berries if available in yard plantings. Phoebes do not nest in boxes, but they are such eager users of ledges, eaves, and rafters that they welcome a nesting shelf with 6-7 inch sides and a sloping roof about 6 inches above the bottom; tack it 8-12 feet up on the side of a building or garden arbor, preferably near water. Phoebes will also feed on blackberries, blueberries, elderberries, hackberries, and sumac fruit in a garden.

SWIFTS, SWALLOWS, AND MARTINS

Chimney Swift (*Chaetura pelagica*), **Purple Martin** (*Progne subis*), **Tree Swallow** (*Tachycineta bicolor*), and **Barn Swallow** (*Hirundo rustica*)

Swifts and swallows have a good deal in common, mostly things related to their aerial lifestyle; they feed, drink, and bathe on the wing, they are found only in open areas where they have the airspace needed for their distinctive rapid, darting flight, and they eat flying insects almost exclusively. The two groups, however, are not at all related. The more primitive swifts are related to hummingbirds; they cannot perch, but cling vertically to walls inside their roosts or nesting chimneys. Swallows and martins are true songbirds, and they can perch on wires or flat surfaces.

Tree Swallows

DISTRIBUTION: All these birds leave their northern breeding grounds in winter, usually for Central or South America. Chimney Swifts breed from the Great Plains east to the Atlantic Coast. Purple Martins occur all across the U.S. except in Alaska and parts of the Rocky Mountains. Tree Swallows nest in all the northern and central states. Barn Swallows breed in southern Alaska and almost all other regions of the U.S.

IDENTIFICATION: Chimney Swifts are about 5 inches long and entirely dark brown with cigar-shaped bodies and long wings. They are almost never seen except when rapidly flying or soaring high overhead as they utter chittering calls. Purple Martins are a bit larger, with long wings but a moderately forked tail; the males are uniformly glossy blue-black, and the females are gray below. The song is a gurgling *tchew-wew.* Tree Swallows are small, and both sexes are glossy blue-green above and white below. Their song is a liquid twitter. Barn Swallows are larger, blue-black above and cinnamon-buff below with a dark red throat. The long forked "swallow tail" is dark blue with white spots.

HABITAT: Swifts occur in open areas and woodlands, especially around human habitation. Martins like open areas too, most frequently grassy river valleys, lake shores, and other open areas near water. Tree Swallows also prefer open situations near water including lakes, ponds, marshes, streams, and coastal regions. Barn Swallows are found over open fields and pastures and very open wooded areas.

DIET: Swifts are entirely insectivorous, and swallows are almost so, catching their prey on the wing. They will eat any insect that flies, especially the small abundant species like mosquitoes and gnats; they will also take airborne spiders. Martins and Tree Swallows will occasionally feed on insects on the ground, and Tree Swallows also eat bayberries and the seeds of bulrushes, sedges, and other plants.

NESTING: Although Chimney Swifts originally nested in natural tree cavities, they now use chimneys or air shafts almost entirely for roosting and nesting. The nest looks like a cup of glued-together twigs that was cut in half and attached to the inside wall of a chimney. Both sexes incubate their 2-7 eggs for 19-21 days, and the young can fly when 30 days old. Purple Martins nest in colonies that can reach incredible numbers. They carry grasses, leaves, mud, feathers, paper, and other materials into the nest box; the female lays 3-8 eggs and incubates them for 15-16 days while the male guards the nest. The young leave about 28 days after hatching. Tree Swallows also nest in cavities, with the female gathering a base of grass and straw and a lining of feathers (preferably white, from chickens) for the nest; the 4-6 eggs are incubated for 13-16

Purple Martins

days, and the young fly 16-24 days later. Barn Swallows commonly build their nests in groups on barn rafters or inside other buildings, under eaves, bridges, or boat docks, or in natural crevices. They form a solid cup of mud pellets and grass with a lining of white poultry feathers or horsehair. The 4-7 eggs are incubated for 13-17 days by both sexes, and the young fly 18-23 days after hatching.

HOW TO ATTRACT: Chimney Swifts cannot be actively attracted, but you can allow them into your yard if you remove any blockage over your chimney in early spring before the birds arrive, and if you do not use your fireplace again until after they have left! Chapter 6 discusses problems that may arise with swifts in a chimney. Martins, of course, can be attracted with nest boxes; Chapter 4 contains details about houses for martin colonies. Tree Swallows will nest in single boxes mounted on a pole 10-15 feet above the ground with clear flying space in front of it. Barn Swallows will use a nesting shelf with 6-inch sides and a sloping roof 6 inches above the floor; set the shelf 8-12 feet up the side of a building.

Barn Swallows

CROWS AND JAYS

American Crow (*Corvus brachyrhynchos*), **Blue Jay** (*Cyanocitta cristata*), and **Scrub Jay** (*Aphelocoma coerulescens*)

Some of the most familiar of American birds, crows and jays are highly intelligent and interesting to watch. If you have large groups of these birds in your area, you might see them "mob" a predator. If one crow or jay finds an owl, a hawk, or a squirrel, he will call to others in the area who then dive, buzz, and chatter at the predator relentlessly and mercilessly, even pursuing it once it has been driven off. This is especially unusual since crows and jays are really too large to be threatened by the predators they usually mob; there is no obvious explanation for the habit. These birds are known to be unmistakably loud and chatty — sometimes to the point of annoyance — and they seem to enjoy picking on other birds, too. Jays are quite colorful, which helps to make up for some of their less admirable habits.

DISTRIBUTION: American Crows range throughout the East and most of the West except for arid parts of the Southwest; they leave the north-central states in winter. Blue Jays are generally found east of the Rocky Mountains; the northernmost birds often move south for a short distance in winter. Scrub Jays have two distinct nonmigratory populations: one in the southwestern quarter of the U.S. extending up to Washington and Oregon, and the other in peninsular Florida.

IDENTIFICATION: American Crows are 17-21 inches and entirely glossy black with a heavy bill; they commonly travel in flocks and their loud *caws* can be heard for long distances. Blue Jays are medium-sized (11-12 inches) and bright blue on the top of the crested head and on the wings, back, and tail (note that their blue can look rather grayish on dark days); they are white below and have a black "necklace"; their most common call is a loud *jay-jay,* but they also have many other sounds, including imitations of hawk screams. Scrub Jays are about the same size as Blue Jays but have a black mask and no crest; they are cobalt blue above with a grayish or brown back, and gray below with a white-streaked breast band that sometimes is edged with blue.

American Crow

HABITAT: Crows occur across the U.S. in almost any habitat where they can find food—woodlands, farms, fields, shores and urban and suburban areas. Blue Jays are more limited, being found in eastern forests, open woodlands, residential areas, and parks with trees. Scrub Jays occur in chaparral, brush areas, and suburbs and in western oak, pinyon, and juniper scrub. There is also a small isolated population of Scrub Jays in the scrub oaklands of Florida, where it is endangered because of habitat loss.

DIET: Crows are truly omnivorous, but they primarily eat corn and other grains; they also feed on insects, birds and their eggs, amphibians, shellfish, small mammals, carrion, and garbage. Blue Jays are omnivorous as well, but mostly feed on acorns, beechnuts, and corn; they also take fruit and insects including beetles, grasshoppers, and gypsy moth caterpillars; their appetite for small birds and eggs is exaggerated—they eat three times as much vegetable matter as animal. Scrub Jays eat acorns and other nuts, grains such as corn, a wide variety of wild and cultivated fruit, insects, and small animals. Although crows and jays commonly bury food, they don't recover all of their stores and some may sprout; these birds are thus responsible for some natural replanting of forests and scrub.

NESTING: Birds in this family construct large and bulky nests of twigs. Crows usually build in tall trees; 3-8 eggs are incubated by both sexes for 18 days and the young fly in 4-5 weeks. Blue Jays often build in the crotch of a tree; 3-6 eggs are incubated mostly by the female for 17-18 days and the young fly in 17-21 days. Normally bold and obvious, Blue Jays become quiet and secretive when they are nesting. Scrub Jays use a shrub or low tree; their 2-7 eggs are incubated by the female for 16 days and the young fly in 18 days. Recent study has proved that young Florida (but not western) Scrub Jays are "cooperative breeders"—they may spend several years helping their parents to feed and raise later brothers and sisters before beginning to nest on their own. Study of crows and Blue Jays indicates that they may do the same thing, although in a more limited way.

HOW TO ATTRACT: If you wish to avoid rather than attract crows, they can be discouraged by making your feeders too small for them to perch on; also, scattering cheaper whole corn or cobs at a distance from the main feeders will usually satisfy crows. Jays are especially fond of sunflower seed, suet, bread, and nuts of all kinds; they can even be trained to come to hand-held food, especially nuts. Jays also make excellent watchdogs, crying out warning to the other birds when predators approach.

Blue Jays

Scrub Jay

CHICKADEES, TITMICE, BUSHTITS, AND NUTHATCHES

Black-capped Chickadee (*Parus atricapillus*), **Tufted Titmouse** (*Parus bicolor*), **Bushtit** (*Psaltriparus minimus*), and **White-breasted Nuthatch** (*Sitta carolinensis*)

These birds are well known for their acrobatics. Chickadees and titmice easily cling in any position to almost anything, from the tips of small branches while they search out tiny insects to your feeders stocked with a favorite food. The western Bushtit is similar in appearance and antics but is not closely related. Nuthatches are larger and not as agile as the others but are notable because of the way they search tree trunk crevices for food — upside down.

DISTRIBUTION: Black-capped Chickadees occur from Alaska south through the central U.S. Tufted Titmice are easterners and range from Minnesota to Texas. Nuthatches are found across the U.S. except Alaska, the northwest coast, and drier parts of the West. Bushtits live along the West Coast and in the Southwest.

IDENTIFICATION: The Black-capped Chickadee is very small (about 4-5 inches) with a gray-and-white body with buffy sides and a black cap and bib; the call is a distinctive *chick-a-dee-dee-dee*. The Tufted Titmouse is 6 inches or a bit larger and gray, with an obvious crest, black forehead, and pinkish flanks; the call is a loud whistled *peter-peter-peter*. The Bushtit is only about 4 inches, gray-brown, with a long tail and short bill; some bushtits have brown or black ear patches; the call is a high-pitched *tsit-tsit-tsit*. The White-breasted Nuthatch is small (5-6 inches) with a gray back, black cap, and white underparts; its voice is a distinctively nasal *yank*. The similar Red-breasted Nuthatch (*Sitta canadensis*) is smaller with a rusty breast and white eye stripe.

HABITAT: These birds are most often found in forests, open woodlands, oak and juniper scrub, chaparral, parks, and suburbs. They have a strong preference for heavily wooded areas, but they are also comfortable in thick, tangled shrub.

Black-capped Chickadee

Tufted Titmouse

White-breasted Nuthatch

Bushtit

DIET: Small insects and spiders and their eggs and larvae, aphids, scale insects, and leafhoppers are the mainstay of their diet; the larger species take caterpillars, moth larvae, wasps, and beetles; in fall and winter they also eat seeds, wild fruit, and nuts.

NESTING: Chickadees, titmice, and nuthatches all nest in holes, usually natural tree cavities or old woodpecker holes. Black-capped Chickadees prefer to be fairly close to the ground, no more than 10 feet up; they lay surprisingly large clutches for so small a bird; 5-10 eggs are incubated by both parents for 11-13 days, and the young fly in 14-18 days. Tufted Titmice usually nest higher in trees; their 4-8 eggs are incubated by the female for 13-14 days; the young fly in 17-18 days. White-breasted Nuthatches also prefer holes in tall trees; they lay 5-10 eggs incubated by both sexes for 12 days, and the young fly about 14 days later. Bushtits differ by building an enormous (for the bird's size) gourd-shaped hanging pocket of twigs, mosses, rootlets, lichens, and spider silk with a hole on one side near the top; they lay 5-13 eggs that are incubated by both sexes for 12 days; the young fly in 14-15 days.

HOW TO ATTRACT: All four species are enthusiastic and tame feeder visitors. Depending on which species occur in the same area in winter, they frequently travel and feed together in small flocks. Chickadees and titmice are especially fond of sunflower seed, suet, doughnuts, and peanuts; they are adept at clinging to small specialized feeders and balls of suet and peanut butter mixtures. With patience, they can often be taught to come to hand-held food. Bushtits will visit feeders for suet, peanut butter mixtures, and doughnuts; they also use birdbaths often. Nuthatches are particularly fond of sunflower seed, suet, and "puddings."

The chickadees, nuthatches, and titmice readily use nest boxes. Set them up 6-10 feet off the ground for chickadees and 10-20 feet up for nuthatches and titmice. These are forest birds; they usually require a heavy patch of trees for nesting, but they might settle for dense shrubs or bushes that resemble a wood's edge if your yard is well stocked.

WRENS

House Wren (*Troglodytes aedon*) and Carolina Wren (*Thryothorus ludovicianus*)

Wrens are familiar little brown birds that move energetically about thickets and brushy areas, usually with their tails cocked at a jaunty angle. Their loud, cheerful voices can be exceptionally musical. The 59 species of wrens are confined to North and South America, except for the Winter Wren (*Troglodytes troglodytes*), which appears in England. Ten species occur in the U.S.

DISTRIBUTION: House Wrens breed all across the U.S except in Alaska and the southernmost tier of states; they migrate into those southern states in the winter. Carolina Wrens are basically nonmigratory southeastern birds, but they do range as far west as Texas and as far north as southern New England.

IDENTIFICATION: House Wrens are very small at about 5 inches and grayish red-brown above, lighter below, with fine dark barring in most of the plumage. The song is an exuberant cascade of bubbling notes that rise and fall. Carolina Wrens are slightly larger, warm reddish brown above and buffy below with the fine barring typical of wrens on their wings and tail; a distinct white eyebrow stripe is set off by a darker line above and below it. The vivacious, melodious song — *teakettle, teakettle, teakettle* — is surprisingly loud for a bird that size.

HABITAT: House Wrens are found in thickets, brushy areas, and shrubbery in open woodlands, orchards, farmlands, chaparral, and suburban gardens. Carolina Wrens occur in open, moist deciduous forests, usually in thickets, underbrush, or swamps, and in wooded parks and suburbs.

Carolina Wren

DIET: Both species are largely insectivorous. House Wrens eat grasshoppers, beetles, caterpillars, ants, bees, wasps, and flies, as well as spiders, snails, and millipedes. Carolina Wrens also feed on boll weevils, stink bugs, leafhoppers, chinch bugs, crane flies, sow bugs, the occasional lizard or frog, and some berries and seeds.

NESTING: Wrens will use almost any kind of cavity for their nests. In addition to natural cavities in rotting trees, old woodpecker holes, and the upturned roots of a fallen tree (a special favorite of Winter Wrens), House Wrens have been known to nest in old shoes, watering cans, flower pots, coffee cans, pump nozzles, iron pipe railings, weather vanes, cars or tractors, teapots, old hats, fishing creels hung in a garage, old nests of other birds like swallows, deserted nests of paper wasps, and empty cow skulls. Carolina Wrens are just as imaginative, having added to the list, stone walls, small baskets, windowsills covered by a heavy growth of ivy, open bags, mailboxes, pockets of clothes (either old ones hanging in a shed, or those drying on a clothesline), and clothespin boxes or bags. Wrens also add industry to their imagination, for the male builds nests in many of the cavities in his territory and the female chooses which cavity (if any) she will use. Even if she selects one of his, she will probably pull out all of his sticks and replace them with ones she has gathered. House Wrens lay 5-9 eggs and incubate them for 13-15 days; the young leave 12-18 days later. Carolina Wrens have similar habits, laying 4-8 eggs that the female incubates for 14 days; the young fledge 13-14 days after hatching.

HOW TO ATTRACT: House Wrens migrate south of their breeding grounds for the winter, but Carolina Wrens are permanent residents, so they are avid winter feeders on suet, peanut butter mixtures, nut bits, sunflower seed, and breads. Both House and Carolina wrens readily use nest boxes, as do the more southern and western Bewick's Wrens (*Thryomanes bewickii*). If the entrance hole is wider than high (like a mailbox slot), it is easier for the birds to get their long sticks into the box.

House Wrens

ROBINS, BLUEBIRDS, MOCKINGBIRDS, AND THRASHERS

American Robin (*Turdus migratorius*), **Eastern Bluebird** (*Sialia sialis*), **Northern Mockingbird** (*Mimus polyglottos*), and **Brown Thrasher** (*Toxostoma rufum*)

Robins and bluebirds are thrushes, and mockingbirds and thrashers belong to the closely related family of mimic thrushes. These familiar birds are all insectivorous during the breeding season but largely fruit-eating the rest of the year.

DISTRIBUTION: American Robins breed throughout the U.S. except for Florida and parts of the Southwest, and in winter they leave the coldest parts of their range such as the north-central states. Eastern Bluebirds breed east of the Rocky Mountains but withdraw from the northern states during winter. Northern Mockingbirds can be found in all but the north-central and northwestern states while breeding, but they leave the northern parts of their range during winter. Brown Thrashers summer east of the Rockies from Montana to Texas, but they occur only in the Southeast during winter.

IDENTIFICATION: American Robins are large, gray to black above and a muddy red below; females are paler. The Robin's song is a clear *cheerily cheer-up cheerio*. Eastern Bluebirds are about 7 inches, bright blue above and brick red below; females are much paler. The bluebird song is a musical *chur chur-lee chur-lee*. The Western Bluebird (*Sialia mexicana*) differs by being deep purple-blue (including on the throat and upper breast) and darker red on the lower breast. Northern Mockingbirds are long, slender gray birds; the darker wings and tail have large white patches. Brown Thrashers look like large thrushes, rusty brown above and brown-streaked below, but with a very long tail. Both are expert mimics of other birds' songs; the Mockingbird is the most skilled and repeats most phrases three times, and the Thrasher sings them twice.

American Robin's nest

Brown Thrasher

HABITAT: Robins occur in forests, woodlands, scrub, parks, thickets, gardens, and farmlands. Bluebirds prefer more open situations such as forest edges, areas with scattered trees, orchards, golf courses, and farmlands. Mockingbirds also are found in many open or partly open regions like scattered brush, forest edges, scrub, parks, and gardens. Thrashers live in forest clearings and edges, thickets, brush, and suburbs.

DIET: Robins specialize on worms, but they also eat insects and wild fruits like grapes, mistletoe berries, pokeberries, dogwood fruit, and bayberries, and cultivated fruits such as strawberries. Bluebirds feed on many insects, including grasshoppers, crickets, katydids, and beetles, and on wild fruit. Mockingbirds love grasshoppers and beetles but also eat many other insects, snails, lizards, and small snakes, and such fruits as holly, smilax, elderberry, pokeberry, and blackberry. Brown Thrashers feed mostly by scratching and digging under leaf litter for June beetles and grubs, Japanese beetles, curculios, caterpillars, and other small insects. They also eat pokeberries and hackberries.

NESTING: Robins build their deep cup nests of mud and grass in sheltered sites; otherwise the mud base would soften in rain. The first nest of the season is usually in a dense evergreen, but deciduous trees are used for the next one or two. Robins may also use a protected spot under eaves, roof gutters, or porch gables. The female lays 3-6 eggs and incubates them for 12-14 days; the spotted young leave the nest 14-16 days later. Bluebirds nest in natural tree cavities, old woodpecker holes, and holes in rail fences. The nest of grasses and other fine materials holds 3-7 eggs incubated by the female for 13-16 days; the young fly after another 15-20 days. Mockingbird pairs build their untidy nest in a small bush, vine tangle, cactus, or small tree. The female incubates the 3-6 eggs for 12 days, and the young fledge 10-12 days later. Thrashers may nest on the ground, but more often in a low shrub or brush pile. The large nest has many layers of dead leaves, twigs, and paper for the 3-6 eggs that are incubated by both sexes for 12-14 days; the young leave in 9-13 days.

HOW TO ATTRACT: All these fruit-eaters will come to feeders for raisins, apple slices and other fruit, peanut butter mixtures, and white bread. They will also eat the fruit in your garden plantings. To have a resident Mockingbird in your yard, you almost have to have trees and shrubs with winter fruit. Robins readily accept nesting shelves with a 6×8-inch floor and a sloping roof 8 inches above the floor. Fasten the shelf 6-15 feet above the ground in a sheltered site on a building or garden arbor. Bluebird populations have greatly benefited from a nationwide effort to provide them with nesting places. Keep an eye on the boxes during early spring to make sure they haven't been taken by House Wrens.

American Robin

Eastern Bluebird

Northern Mockingbird

FINCHES AND GROSBEAKS

Northern Cardinal (*Cardinalis cardinalis*), **House Finch** (*Carpodacus mexicanus*), **American Goldfinch** (*Carduelis tristis*), and **Evening Grosbeak** (*Coccothraustes vespertinus*)

At first glance, these birds may not look similar, but they all have heavy, seed-cracking bills and are actually closely related. All are familiar species at feeders in winter, but your budding shrubs and trees will be of more interest to them during breeding season.

American Goldfinch

DISTRIBUTION: Despite their name, Northern Cardinals are basically southern and eastern birds, occurring from North Dakota down to Texas and across the Southwest to California. House Finches are common throughout the West and have been introduced in the East, now ranging from the Atlantic coast into the Great Plains. American Goldfinches breed across the northern half of the U.S., except for Alaska; they spend the winter in the southern part of their nesting range and in the southern U.S. Evening Grosbeaks breed in the western mountains, across southern Canada and northern Minnesota to New England. In some winters, they are seen in large numbers throughout the U.S.

IDENTIFICATION: The cardinal male is 8 inches long, brilliant red with a large crest and a black face and chin; his mate is buffy yellow-brown with a red crest, wings, and tail; the songs are cheerful whistles, *pret-ty-pret-ty-pret-ty.* The House Finch is small (5-6 inches) and brown-striped; the male has orangy-red eyebrows, upper breast, and rump, and brown-streaked sides; the song is long, disjointed, and cheerful. House Finches are easily confused with Purple Finches (*Carpodacus purpureus*), which differ by being rosy red without side streaks in the male, and having a distinct facial pattern in the female. The small 5-inch male American Goldfinch, often called a "wild canary," is unmistakable in his summer plumage of bright yellow with black cap, wings, and tail; in winter he looks like a female, dull brownish olive; goldfinch flight is distinctively undulating and usually accompanied by the flight call, *per-chick-o-ree.* Evening Grosbeaks are large (7-8½ inches), with powerful yellowish or lime-green bills; the male is black, white, and yellow, and the female is smoke gray with black-and-white wings and tail; the call is a strident *clee-ip.*

HABITAT: These birds breed in quite different habitats, but all will frequent suburbs in winter. Cardinals like thickets, brushy fields, forest edges, and clearings. House Finches are native to the West, where they live in semiarid habitats, suburbs, and cities. In the 1940s, they were introduced to the East and have spread so rapidly that they are now considered pests in some areas. Goldfinches prefer weedy fields, cultivated lands, and open woodlands. Evening Grosbeaks breed in spruce-fir forests and mixed woodlands; they winter in forests, woodlands, and suburbs.

DIET: The specialized bills of these species allow them to eat many different kinds of seeds in winter, but they feed on a wide variety of insects, wild berries, weed seeds, and buds in summer. The smaller finches specialize on thistle and dandelion seed.

NESTING: Cardinals build a bowl-shaped nest of twigs and weed stems in a dense shrub or thicket; 2-6 eggs are incubated mostly by the female for 12-13 days; the young leave the nest in 10-11 days.

Evening Grosbeak

Northern Cardinal

House Finches nest in cavities, buildings, or dense vegetation; their 2-6 eggs are incubated for 12-16 days, and the young leave the nest 11-19 days after hatching. Goldfinches breed later than most songbirds, when thistle and milkweed down is available for building a tightly woven cup nest; 4-6 eggs are incubated by the female for 12-14 days; the young are fed entirely on seeds regurgitated by their parents and leave the nest at 10-16 days old. Evening Grosbeaks are gregarious even when nesting and may breed in loose colonies; they build a shallow cup of twigs, usually high in a spruce; 2-5 eggs are incubated by the female, probably for 12-14 days; the young leave the nest in 13-14 days.

HOW TO ATTRACT: These are the sunflower-seed specialists. Evening Grosbeak bills are probably the most efficient sunflower-seed huskers of all time. Grosbeaks have expensive tastes and they don't appear in all parts of their range every year, but a crowd of these gorgeous nomads at your feeder may be the winter's highlight in enjoyment. Cardinals are fond of sunflower and safflower seed, but they and House Finches will eat almost any seed, corn, nuts, or bread. In spite of their size, cardinals can be surprisingly intimidated at feeders by smaller species like goldfinches. Goldfinches like sunflower seed, peanuts, and other nut meats, but they favor thistle, thistle, and more thistle! Often joining in the goldfinch quarrels at thistle and sunflower-seed feeders are their close relatives, Pine Siskins (*Carduelis pinus*), which have varying degrees of yellow in the wing and tail base, but otherwise are heavily streaked brown and white. House Finches are quite relaxed in their choice of nest sites and they use nest boxes; you have a good chance of enticing a pair to nest.

House Finch

SPARROWS, JUNCOS, AND TOWHEES

Chipping Sparrow (*Spizella passerina*), **Song Sparrow** (*Melospiza melodia*), **White-crowned Sparrow** (*Zonotrichia leucophrys*), **Dark-eyed Junco** (*Junco hyemalis*), and **California Towhee** (*Pipilo crissalis*)

Many generally small, generally brown birds will gather at feeders, and identifying them can be a challenge because they appear so similar. If the birds that visit your feeders don't seem to be listed in this book, they may be American Tree Sparrows (*Spizella arborea*), Brewer's Sparrows (*S. breweri*), Field Sparrows (*S. pusilla*), Fox Sparrows (*Passerella iliaca*), White-throated Sparrows (*Zonotrichia albicollis*), Rufous-sided Towhees (*Pipilo erythrophthalmus*), or Green-tailed Towhees (*P. chlorurus*), depending on your region.

Chipping Sparrow

Dark-eyed Junco

DISTRIBUTION: Chipping Sparrows nest in all regions of the U.S., but they winter only in the southern states. Song Sparrows are similar except that their breeding range excludes most of the southern Great Plains and southeastern states. White-crowned Sparrows nest across Alaska and northern Canada and down the western Rockies to California and New Mexico; they spend the winter in the Northwest and in the southern half of the country except for the southeastern coast. Dark-eyed Juncos breed across Alaska and Canada and most regions between the West Coast and the eastern Rocky Mountains; in winter they can be found almost anywhere in the continental U.S. California Towhees are permanent residents of California and Oregon.

IDENTIFICATION: All the sparrows are generally brown above and lighter below. Chipping Sparrows are about 5 inches with a chestnut crown and white eye stripe; in winter, the crown is streaked and grayish buff. The song is a rapid trill of *chips*. Song Sparrows are larger (up to 7 inches) with a streaked breast that has a central "stickpin" spot; their lovely song is a series of three or four clear notes followed by a trill. White-crowned Sparrows reach 7 inches and have a distinctly black-and-white striped head; the song varies — a few thin whistles followed by a trill. Dark-eyed Juncos are a bit smaller and basically gray or gray-brown, but their coloring is extremely varied; they all have white feathers in the tail and sing with a single-pitched musical trill. California Towhees are the largest of the group at 8½-10 inches; they are brown with a long tail, and their song varies.

Song Sparrow

Song Sparrow's nest

White-crowned Sparrow

HABITAT: All these birds frequent suburban parks and yards in winter, but they like to stay in or near brushy, scrubby thickets. In summer, they breed in different habitats, from mountain forests and meadows to coastal marshes.

DIET: Chipping Sparrows eat a great many grass seeds; they also feed on small insects and spiders. Song Sparrows rely more on insects, but they also eat grass and weed seeds and wild fruit. White-crowned Sparrows specialize on weed seeds, some insects, and odd items like moss fruiting bodies and willow catkins. In summer, juncos feed heavily on insects and on tree seeds, relying on weed and grass seeds the rest of the year. Towhees eat weed and grass seeds and insects.

NESTING: In these species, the female builds the nest and incubates the eggs; the male usually then helps to feed the nestlings. Chipping Sparrows build a neat little cup of grasses, usually in a dense tree close to the ground; their 3-5 eggs are incubated for 11-14 days, and the young fledge 8-12 days later. Song Sparrows usually nest on the ground in a clump of grass; 3-6 eggs are incubated for 12-13 days, and the young leave the nest in about 10 days, often before they can fly. White-crowned Sparrows build a bulky cup of twigs and grasses, usually on the ground in a well-concealed spot; the 3-5 eggs are incubated for 11-16 days, and the young leave 10 days later. Juncos form a deep cup of mosses and twigs in a sheltered area near the ground. The 3-6 eggs are incubated for 11-12 days, and the young leave when 12-13 days old. Towhees usually nest a few feet above the ground in a dense bush or tree; 2-6 eggs are incubated for 11 days, and the young are only 8 days old when they fledge.

HOW TO ATTRACT: As is evident from their natural histories, these birds stay on or near the ground and mostly eat small seeds. At feeders, they prefer to eat seed, especially white millet, but also sunflower that other species have knocked to the ground. If cats are not in the area, Song Sparrows may use a 6×6-inch nesting shelf with a roof 6 inches over the floor, placed 1-3 feet above the ground.

BLACKBIRDS AND ORIOLES

Red-winged Blackbird (*Agelaius phoeniceus*), **Brown-headed Cowbird** (*Molothrus ater*), **Common Grackle** (*Quiscalus quiscula*), and **Northern Oriole** (*Icterus galbula*)

These members of the blackbird family have somewhat different habits, and they look quite different, especially the oriole. They are grouped together because they all have the same conical, sharply pointed bill and flat, "Roman-nosed" profile.

DISTRIBUTION: Red-winged Blackbirds breed throughout the U.S. including Alaska and spend the winter in all but the northernmost states. Brown-headed Cowbirds frequent all of the U.S. except Alaska during the breeding season, and they winter in the East and Southwest. Common Grackles occur east of the Rocky Mountains in summer, but they abandon the northwestern parts of that range during the winter. Northern Orioles breed over most of the U.S. except Alaska and the Southeast; a few birds spend the winter in the southernmost states, but the majority migrate to the tropics.

IDENTIFICATION: Red-winged Blackbirds are medium-sized (7-9 inches) songbirds; the male is glossy black with brilliant red shoulder patches edged in yellow; the female and young are dark brown above, heavily streaked brown and white below; the song is a loud *konk-la-ree*. Brown-headed Cowbirds are smaller (6-8 inches); the male is black with a brown head, and the female is sooty gray-brown; the spring song is a gurgling *glug-glug-gleee*. Common Grackles are larger (11-13½ inches) and have a long tail and iridescent purple or bronze on the head, neck, and back; their call is a loud *chack*. Northern Orioles (7-8 inches) are very different, with the males a flaming orange and black with some white in the black wing; females vary from dull gray to brownish-olive above, pale orange or yellow below; oriole songs are musical, two-noted whistles.

Northern Oriole

Common Grackle

HABITAT: Red-wings are birds of freshwater and brackish marshes, sloughs, areas with small trees and brush near water, and cultivated lands and pastures. Cowbirds prefer woodlands, forest edges, farmlands, streamsides, marshes, and towns. The Common Grackle frequents groves, towns, and farmlands. A larger (16-17 inches) species, the Boat-Tailed Grackle (*Quiscalus major*) is found in coastal habitats from New York to Texas; the very similar Great-tailed Grackle (*Q. mexicanus*) occurs on the coast and is expanding inland from Louisiana to interior California. Orioles differ from the other blackbirds by being treetop birds; they are found in open woodlands, orchards, river groves, and shade trees.

DIET: Blackbirds are fairly omnivorous, feeding especially on weed seeds and waste grain, with grasshoppers and other insects and small invertebrates in summer. Grackles are even less picky, also eating fish and frogs and the eggs and young of small birds. Orioles specialize on caterpillars and a variety of other small insects, but they also love fruit and nectar so you might be able to entice them down from the treetops.

NESTING: Red-wings weave their nests in cattails or reeds, often near water but also in upland fields; 3-5 eggs are incubated by the female for 11-12 days; the young can climb out of the nest in about 10 days. Cowbirds are nest parasites like the Common (European) Cuckoo (*Cuculus canorus*). A female cowbird builds no nest, but lays 10-12 eggs (total) in the nests of smaller species like vireos, warblers, and sparrows. She leaves her egg for the host to incubate it for 11-14 days; the young cowbird usually flies in about 19 days and often is the only youngster raised in that brood. Grackles breed in tall shade trees or marshes, singly or in colonies; the nests are bulky but compact masses of twigs and grass stalks, sometimes with a mud base; 4-7 eggs are incubated by the female for 13-14 days and the young fly in 18-20 days. Orioles build a soft, distinctive nest of plant fibers, hair, and string, hung from a branch tip of a tall tree; 4-6 eggs are incubated for 12-14 days; the young fly in another 12-14 days.

HOW TO ATTRACT: Blackbirds eat almost anything, especially grains, breads, and suet. Because they travel in large flocks in winter, their sheer numbers can be a nuisance at feeders. When a female oriole is building a nest, she will use colored pieces of yarn or cloth and hair put out in the yard; orioles also readily come to feeders for fruit, sugar water, and mixtures of suet and peanut butter. Some Northern Orioles now more commonly spend the winter in the northern part of their range because of the food available at feeders. The Hooded Oriole (*Icterus cucullatus*) of the Southwest also comes to feeders for sugar water and fruit.

Red-winged Blackbird

Brown-headed Cowbird

PEST SPECIES

Rock Dove (*Columba livia*), European Starling (*Sturnus vulgaris*), and House Sparrow (*Passer domesticus*)

These birds are treated as a group not because they are related to each other, but because they have developed huge populations and are now considered agricultural and urban pests.

House Sparrow

DISTRIBUTION: Rock Doves, European Starlings, and House Sparrows now live in virtually every part of the U.S. that people do.

IDENTIFICATION: Rock Doves are the large (13-14 inch) city pigeons. Most are predominantly dark gray with a white rump and some iridescence on the neck; they may also be entirely white, rusty brown, or with mixtures of those colors and gray. The voice is a guttural cooing. The smaller European Starlings are iridescent black with brown wings, a short tail, and a yellow bill. The young birds are gray-brown. Adults in fall have white tips on their black feathers; the tips gradually wear off, so the birds lose their spangled appearance by early spring. Starling calls are mostly whistles; they also mimic the songs of other species. House Sparrows (also called English Sparrows) are 6-inch brown birds; the male has a gray cap, chestnut neck, white cheeks, and a black bib, whereas the female is plain buffy brown. The call is a monotonous chirping.

HABITAT: Rock Doves originally nested on rocky cliffs as a wild species but now are almost entirely associated with humans, especially in cities and suburbs. They also occur on farms if nesting sites are available. Starlings and House Sparrows nest in cavities and may be found anywhere there are humans and places to nest — cities, suburbs, forested areas, and farmlands.

DIET: Rock Doves feed primarily on seeds and grains, but also some insects, buds, and garbage. Starlings eat many harmful insects, especially Japanese beetles, grubs, cutworms, clover weevils, and grasshoppers; they also eat weed seeds, grain, garbage, and wild fruit. They are pests on cultivated fruit and sometimes grain when they accompany large winter flocks of native blackbirds. In addition, their droppings cause disease and sanitation problems at their huge winter roosts. House Sparrows also eat a great many insect pests such as Japanese beetles, click beetles, leaf beetles, and caterpillars, as well as crab grass and other weed seeds, waste grain, and garbage.

NESTING: Rock Doves lay 1-2 eggs on a messy platform of twigs and sticks on a building ledge, rafter, or bridge beam. If a better site is not available, they may nest on the ground in secure surroundings. Both sexes incubate the eggs for 17-19 days; the chicks leave the nest after 35-37 days. Starlings compete successfully with native birds like Common Flickers, Great Crested Flycatchers, bluebirds, and swallows for nesting cavities. Both sexes incubate the 2-8 eggs for 12 days, and the young fly 21 days later. House Sparrow males guard their nest cavity year-round. Nest sites may be anywhere — crevices in buildings, natural tree holes, on rafters, behind shutters, under eaves, in traffic lights. Even if the cavity is large, it is filled to overflowing with grass, straw, and other

materials. Occasionally House Sparrows will nest in trees, constructing a large dome-shaped ball of straw and grass with a side entrance. The 3-7 eggs are incubated mostly by the female for 11-14 days, and the young leave in 15-17 days.

HOW TO AVOID: These three species can be feeder nuisances when they visit in large flocks and consume a lot of food. See Chapter 6 for ideas on how to discourage feeder pests. Starlings can be excluded from any nest box with a hole smaller than 2 inches. If, however, they are chasing a pair of flickers or flycatchers out of a box, the only solution is to put up more boxes so there will be enough to go around. Starlings and House Sparrows can be kept out of martin houses by blocking the holes until the martins reappear in spring; the pests begin nesting earlier than martins do. Sparrows will usually stay away from bluebird boxes if the boxes are no higher than 5 feet above the ground, and if they do not have a perch. If that doesn't work, try cutting the hole as a rectangle, 1½ inches high, but only 1¼ inches wide; bluebirds are slimmer than House Sparrows.

European Starling

Rock Dove

Distribution and Food Preferences for Common North American Birds

Species	Northeast	Southeast	Northwest	Southwest	Beef Suet	Breads	Seeds and Grains	Nuts*	Fruit
Blackbird, Red-winged	●	●	●	●	●	●	■	●	●
Blackbird, Yellow-headed	●		●	●			■		
Bluebird, Eastern	●	●			●	●		●	■
Bluebird, Western			●	●				●	■
Bobwhite, Northern	●	●				●	■		●
Bunting, Indigo	●	●		●			■	●	●
Bushtit			●	●	■			●	
Cardinal, Northern	●	●		●		●	■	●	
Catbird, Gray	●	●			●	●		●	■
Chat, Yellow-breasted	●	●	●	●				●	■
Chickadee, Black-capped	●		●		●	●	■	●	●
Cowbird, Brown-headed	●	●	●	●		●	■	●	●
Creeper, Brown	●	●	●	●	■	●		●	
Crossbill, Red	●	●	●	●			■		
Crow, American	●	●	●	●	●	●	■	●	●
Dove, Inca				●			■		
Dove, Mourning	●	●	●	●			■		
Dove, Rock	●	●	●	●		●	■	●	
Finch, House	●	●	●	●		●	■	●	●
Finch, Purple	●	●	●	●			■	●	●
Flicker, Northern	●	●	●	●	■	●		●	
Goldfinch, American	●	●	●	●	●		■	●	
Goldfinch, Lesser			●	●			■	●	
Grackle, Common	●	●			●	●	■	●	●
Grosbeak, Blue	●	●	●	●			■		
Grosbeak, Evening	●	●	●	●			■		
Grosbeak, Pine	●		●				■		●
Grouse, Ruffed	●		●				■		
Jay, Blue	●	●			●	●	■	●	●
Jay, Scrub		●	●	●	●	●	■	●	
Jay, Steller's			●	●		●	■	●	
Junco, Dark-eyed	●		●	●	●	●	■	●	
Kinglet, Golden-crowned	●	●	●	●	■			●	
Kinglet, Ruby-crowned	●	●	●	●	■	●		●	
Meadowlark, Eastern	●	●		●			■		

Northern Mockingbird

Northern Bobwhite

Species	Northeast	Southeast	Northwest	Southwest	Beef Suet	Breads	Seeds and Grains	Nuts*	Fruit
Mockingbird, Northern	●	●		●	●	●		●	■
Nuthatch, Red-breasted	●	●	●	●	●		■	●	
Nuthatch, White-breasted	●	●	●	●	●	●	■	●	
Oriole, Northern	●	●	●	●	●			●	■
Pheasant, Ring-necked	●		●			●	■		
Quail, California			●	●			■		
Quail, Gambel's				●			■		
Robin, American	●	●	●	●	●	●		●	■
Sapsucker, Yellow-bellied	●	●	●	●	■	●			
Siskin, Pine	●	●	●	●	●		■	●	
Sparrow, American Tree	●		●	●	●		■	●	
Sparrow, Chipping	●	●	●	●		●	■		
Sparrow, House	●	●	●	●		●	■	●	
Sparrow, Song	●	●	●	●		●	■	●	
Sparrow, White-crowned	●	●	●	●		●	■	●	●
Sparrow, White-throated	●	●		●	●		■		
Starling, European	●	●	●	●	●	■	●	●	●
Tanager, Scarlet	●	●				●		●	■
Tanager, Summer		●		●		●		●	■
Tanager, Western			●	●		●		●	■
Thrasher, Brown	●	●			●	■	●	●	●
Thrush, Hermit	●	●	●	●	●	●		●	■
Thrush, Varied			●	●				●	■
Thrush, Wood	●	●							■
Titmouse, Tufted	●	●			●	●	■	●	
Towhee, California				●			■	●	●
Towhee, Rufous-sided	●	●	●	●	●	●	■		●
Turkey, Wild	●	●	●	●			■		
Warbler, Orange-crowned		●	●	●	■	●		●	●
Warbler, Yellow-rumped	●	●	●	●	■	●		●	●
Waxwing, Cedar	●	●	●	●					■
Woodpecker, Downy	●	●	●	●	■	●		●	
Woodpecker, Hairy	●	●	●	●	■	●	●	●	●
Woodpecker, Pileated	●	●	●		■			●	
Woodpecker, Red-bellied	●	●			■	●		●	●
Wren, Carolina	●	●			■	●	●	●	●
Wren, House	●	●	●	●	■	●		●	

American Robin

Ring-necked Pheasant

Eastern Screech-owl

INDEX